About the Author

Paul B. Kidd is a Sydney-based author, photo-journalist, magazine editor, Radio 2UE talk-back broadcaster and freelance *60 Minutes* researching producer who specialises in true crime, fishing, humour and adventure.

Paul's articles, interviews and photographs have appeared in most Australian major outdoors and men's publications and in numerous magazines and websites worldwide.

Paul B. Kidd is the past editor of *Fishing News*, *The Shimano Yearbook*, *The Tackle Trader* and *Rex Hunt's Fishing Australia Monthly* and is a recognised authority on Australia's waterways and the creatures that inhabit them. He is also an authority on Australian serial killers and criminals who have been sentenced to life imprisonment, never to be released.

Paul is the author of ten books and lives in Sydney's eastern suburbs with his boys Charlie and Dick.

Great
Australian
Fishing Stories

Paul B. Kidd

ABC
Books

For my two mates at my two favourite restaurants.
Peter Doyle Jnr at Doyle's at Watson's Bay and
Tony Tzenos at the Eighteen Foot Sailing Club in Double Bay.
I write about 'em. They cook 'em. Yummo – the best.

Published by ABC Books for the
AUSTRALIAN BROADCASTING CORPORATION
GPO Box 9994 Sydney NSW 2001

Copyright © Paul B. Kidd 2003

First published November 2003

National Library of Australia
Cataloguing-in-Publication data
Kidd, Paul B. (Paul Benjamin), 1945– .
    Great Australian fishing stories.

    ISBN 0 7333 1309 4.

    1. Fishing — Australia — Anecdotes.
    I. Australian Broadcasting Corporation.
    II. Title.

799.10994

Designed by Andrew Cunningham, Studio Pazzo
Typeset in 11.5pt Garamond 3
Prepress by Colorwize, Adelaide
Printed in Australia by Griffin Press, Adelaide

5 4 3 2 1

Contents

A Tall Tale of Tagged Trout

*This tale was told to me many years ago by an
old-timer who wouldn't reveal his source or the
origin of the story, but he believed it to be true.
Despite all of my inquiries, I couldn't find anyone
who knew anything about a four-day Fish Festival
in the district, either still running or in the past,
with tagged trout.*

The annual four-day Fish Festival was shaping up to be a beauty. The big cash prizes on offer were attracting anglers from all over the country, and although there were some notorious cheats among them, the organisers didn't seem to care.

With around 5000 anglers at $10 a pop, they stood to make a killing, so a little fudging here and there wouldn't hurt. In fact the rules almost encouraged it. The boundaries were anywhere within 30 kilometres of the starting point and they weren't policed. The area included four dams and several rivers.

The big prizes were for the capture of Terry the Tagged Trout. There were four Terrys – one for each dam. They were trout from the local trout farm and each had been branded with an identifying tag stapled to its tail.

Amid much fuss and press coverage, each year the Terrys were released into their new homes the day before the event. The release spots were kept secret so as not to give anyone an advantage.

The four Terrys were worth $50,000 each, and even the village idiot could tell you that the organisers were in deep trouble if they were all captured. For that matter, if even one were taken it would prove embarrassing. Plus there were prizes of $10,000 each for the biggest Murray cod and yellowbelly.

You didn't need a degree in mathematics to work out that the difference in prize money on offer and the entry fees collected was minus $170,000 – and that was without running costs. There had to be some skulduggery afoot. The organisers maintained that the prize money for a Terry was underwritten by a big insurance company. But it wasn't, because they knew that a tagged trout would never be caught.

In the five years of the Fish Fest no one had ever caught a Terry, and the organisers had walked away with a bundle every year. To ensure that no one came up with the goods, the Terrys were all orally fed a slow-acting poison before release. While they looked healthy enough when photographed being thrown into the dam, they were as stiff as a board in a matter of hours.

What the organisers did not count on was one of their own being more corrupt than them. He was known as the Moth, because he was attracted to the light. He would get legless at the fishing club or the local and stagger home. If he saw a light on, he would invite himself in for a drink and there was no getting rid of him. He was a dreadful pest drunk, but sober he wasn't a bad bloke at all.

Being an official assistant organiser and Terry-releaser, the Moth had been entrusted with the secrets of the villainy that went on. For his silence, he picked up a small share of the returns. But the Moth had got into big trouble on the punt recently, and with the heavies breathing down his neck for the money, he decided to out-cheat the cheats.

The only bloke he could trust with his life was an old mate of his in Sydney called Bill 'Dago' Oliver. They called him Dago because he never stopped whingeing about the fact that his missus spent her entire life in

front of the TV watching the soapies. It had been going on for years and his constant grizzle was: 'There's not a day goes by without her watching that crap. There's not a day goes by when she does anythin' around the house. There's not a day goes by when I get a meal at home. Fair dinkum, there's not a day goes by ...'

Rocket scientists these two were not. But between them, the Dago and the Moth devised a scheme that would scoop the pool ...

Now the rules of the tournament were loose, but a couple were hard and fast. There was absolutely no berleying allowed before the event and all fish had to be weighed by 6 pm sharp. Apart from that, it was open slather.

'We'll wrap up the cod and yellowbelly sections,' the Moth had told Dago on the phone. 'I know an old cod hole about 50 kilometres out of town. When you arrive a day before the comp, I'll have 'em boilin' on the surface. Oh! And don't forget to bring your snorkel and flippers. You'll need them to catch Terry.'

The Moth drove out to the cod hole, which was on a big corner in a bend in the river, and hung six sheep heads from the branch of an overhanging tree. He made sure to keep them well hidden within the leaves.

He returned a week later to find his self-berleying device working a treat. The sheep's heads were well and truly flyblown and the maggots were dropping into the water at a steady pace.

A week later every fish within 100 kilometres was waiting underneath the tree with its head sticking out of the water and mouth open. He knew that the smaller fish, the redfin and silver perch, would attract the bigger cod and yellowbellies, which would eat them all — then Dago could catch them the first day of the comp at his leisure.

Snookering Terry the Tagged Trout wasn't so simple. It wasn't until four days before the comp that the Moth and Dago devised a plan. And even then it was by a stroke of luck.

To add some authenticity to their shonky contest, the organisers announced that because they were being hounded by cheating anglers with binoculars, they would now release the four Terrys secretly, without any press in attendance. The media spewed. 'How do we know you will release any fish at all?' they barked.

Amid cries of deception and fraud, the organisers agreed to let the media photograph the four boats leaving with the Terrys on board, and also arranged for a trusted observer to go out with each fish releaser.

The observers were selected from the town's most prominent and honest citizens – the Police Chief, the school Principal, the head of the Chamber of Commerce and the Mayor. The Moth couldn't believe his luck. He drew his old mate the Mayor, Alderman Clarrie 'Carbuncle' Carr.

The Mayor was as bald as Yul Brynner and they called him Carbuncle because he was shiny on the outside and full of shit on the inside.

Carbuncle loved nothing better than a bottle of Scotch and a friendly ear. The Moth had such an ear. It would be no trouble to get Carbuncle well and truly under the weather and carry out his deception.

At the releasing of the Terrys on the eve of the comp, the cameras flashed as Carbuncle and the Moth held their Terry up in his plastic bag for all to see. 'Take your time,' the organisers had told the Moth. 'Don't make it obvious where you're heading to let the trout go. And don't let Carbuncle see you give it the poison. Otherwise we'll be paying him blackmail forever.'

The Moth putt-putted a couple of kilometres around the lake before he pulled in at Knot's Pier for the couple of bottles of Scotch he had hidden there the previous day. He primed Carbuncle with one and it wasn't long before the Mayor was dribbling and talking about all the kickbacks he'd taken over the years.

The Moth then loaded a block of concrete with a wire handle on board, explaining to his drunken friend that it was ballast in case a breeze came up. And off they went.

They went straight to Mackenzie's Flats, the shallowest and sandiest part of the dam, where no one had caught a fish in years. Here the Moth tied a hundred metres of sash cord to the concrete block and lowered it over the side. When it hit the bottom a few metres down, he removed the Terry from its bag, tied the other end of the sash cord through its gills,

stuffed the poison capsule up its rear end and threw it overboard for Dago to find in the morning.

Carbuncle was oblivious to all of this because he was out cold in the bottom of the boat. The Moth got stuck into the other bottle of Scotch, and by the time Carbuncle woke from his drunken stupor, the Moth was skiting about the exact location of the maggot-berleyed cod hole, the tethered trout and how clever he and Dago were.

The cunning old mayor, now sober, listened intently.

When the cops hauled the Moth in the following day and questioned him about the body they had found, a body that had apparently drowned

A tagged 'Terry' was worth $50,000 to the lucky angler.

when it got tangled up in a length of sash cord at Mackenzie's Flats, he denied any knowledge of it.

Apparently the victim, complete with flippers and snorkel, had been diving towards the bottom and had become entangled in the cord, because whoever had tied the fish to the end of it had jammed something up its backside, causing it to blow up with air and float to the top.

That explains why they told me ten times to shove the poison capsule down its gob, the Moth thought to himself as he examined the trout the police had found attached to the sash cord.

But where's the tag? he thought to himself. The Moth was puzzled and upset. His partner in crime was dead and the tag was missing. What was going on? 'Had he and Carbuncle seen anything that night?' the police continued. After all, they had headed out in that direction.

'No, sir,' the Moth replied and Carbuncle backed him up.

The cops didn't connect the Moth with the late Dago Oliver and Carbuncle wasn't saying anything. By a strange coincidence, the brother of the guy who found Dago's body, who by an even stranger coincidence happened to be Carbuncle's nephew, turned in a Terry that very afternoon and claimed the fifty grand.

Because the tag was just stuck to the tail, not stapled on like the originals, and the trout was a lot smaller than the original Terrys, the organisers smelt a giant rat, but they couldn't do a thing about it. They had to fork out the money.

And by an even more extraordinary coincidence, Carbuncle's son weighed in a huge cod and a yellowbelly that same day and picked up a cool twenty grand. No one could figure out why maggots kept dropping out of the fishes' gobs at the weigh-in. The organisers were out of pocket, and the cops had an unexplained corpse. Carbuncle came into a lot of money all of a sudden and the Moth left town.

They say he's been sighted around Bondi, where the lights are on 24 hours a day.

A Grand Tale

Anglers from all over the world come to Cairns each year to catch giant marlin with beaks like baseball bats and eyes the size of bread and butter plates. But few of these anglers intend to kill the fish, rather choosing to release them unharmed after the fight. One angler did intend to take a monster marlin and mount it in his den. I went along for the ride; if we caught one, it was my job to kill it ...

It was a big fish. No, not big – huge. And if it wasn't for its 1 metre sickle tail slicing the water about 5 metres back from the bait, we probably wouldn't have known it was there, as we were trolling 'blind' into the sun, with the glare on the water.

But it was there, and by the way it was crawling all over our scad bait, we were in for some hot action. I looked at the skipper on the flying bridge for a second opinion.

'She's a horse,' he mumbled. 'Hope the bastard eats.' It did. If we got it alongside the boat, it was my job to kill it.

I was crewing on a special charter out of Cairns with the world-famous black marlin skipper Captain Dennis 'Brazakka' Wallace. I had

Captain Dennis 'Brazakka' Wallace, world-renowned giant black marlin fisherman.

met and fished with Brazakka 25 years earlier in a Cairns light-tackle tournament and we had become good friends. Legend has it that he was raised by the local Aborigines, and that his nickname is Koori for 'wild man'. I never bothered to find out if that was true. The legend suited me just fine.

We maintained our friendship over the years while pursuing our fishing careers – but going in different directions. I chose to write about my passion, while Brazakka became one of the world's best black marlin captains.

In a career spanning 25 years he has captured or tagged and released thousands of black marlin, including more than 100 of these mightiest of all warriors that weighed in excess of the benchmark 1000 pounds.

Brazakka chartered for and became like a son to the late Lee Marvin. Over 12 seasons they weighted 13 granders and tagged at least a dozen more. One was a bewildering 1320 pounder. That's a lot of sashimi!

Brazakka and I kept in touch, and whenever I was in Cairns or he was in Sydney, we'd get together for a beer. So it came as no great surprise when he rang and asked if I'd like to spend 10 days with him out on the Great Barrier Reef during peak marlin time. Of course I would! But what was the catch?

His charter, a Texan, wanted to take a big fish. He had fished with Brazakka for five seasons and had released hundreds of fish, including a few that would have been more than a grand. This season he wanted to kill one and have it mounted on his wall.

He figured that if the Japanese longliners could take 800,000 assorted billfish out of the ocean each year, then his one fish wasn't going to have a dramatic effect.

As he hadn't killed a marlin in eight years and he required the services of only one deckhand to let them go, he was in a spot. His deckie would be very busy holding the huge fish on the wire leader as it was brought within range of a gaff, and they would need a second man to perform the coup de grâce. I would be that second man.

This moment of mayhem is the most dangerous part of the saga; it is known as 'the kill'. It is when bones are broken, reputations are smashed, and wire and gaff men are often dragged over the side. I've gaffed tiger and mako sharks up to 800 pounds, and they are a handful, but the biggest marlin I've gaffed was no bigger than 300 pounds.

However, I'm a notorious boat slut and would do anything for a ride, let alone 10 days out on the reef, so I accepted immediately, knowing there was always the slim possibility that they might not catch a whopper and my services wouldn't be required.

I could just snap away with my camera, get lots of stories and classic pics and live it up at night on the mothership. Yes, I'd love to go to Cairns.

Actually the term 'fishing at Cairns' is a myth. Fishing 'out of Cairns' would be more accurate. When an expatriate Yank, George Bransford, put Cairns on the map in late 1966 with Richard Obach's 1064 pound black marlin – taken on an 80 pound breaking strain line, to become the first grander taken anywhere in the world since Cabo Blanco in Peru in the early 1950s and the first thousand pounder ever taken on 80 pound line – Bransford's tiny *Sea Baby I* represented half of the Cairns gamefishing fleet.

They would day-trip the 48 kilometres or so out to the reef at an agonisingly slow 10 to 12 knots, punching into a southeast trade wind. They would return with their fish at night and weigh them on the huge scales at the end of the marlin wharf for all to see.

This restricted Bransford to the reefs adjacent to Cairns – either Jennie Louise or Euston. Here the Continental Shelf drops off into a bottomless abyss and the water changes colour from a pissy green to inky onyx in a matter of metres.

It is in this warm water that the giant female black marlin congregate between August and November each year to lay their eggs. The smaller males, fish up to 350 pounds, are in hot pursuit trying to fertilise them; this is what has led to this spawning period being labelled the 'hot bite'.

Why the black marlin choose this area alone to spawn remains a mystery. It could be the abundance of baitfish that gather along the Continental Shelf, the rich vegetation and crustacean-encrusted wall that runs the length of Australia's eastern seaboard.

The baitfish – such as scad, tuna, mahi-mahi, mackerel, wahoo and rainbow runners – attract the giant fish, which in turn create by far the best black marlin fishing ground in the world. More thousand-pound fish are caught here in a week than in all of the world's other hot spots combined in a year.

And so, as word of Bransford's extraordinary catch spread, charter boats and anglers flocked to the area, captures increased and the sportfishing fleet grew, as captains looked further afield for the big fish.

Among other unfished areas, their travels took them to the Ribbon Reefs that stretch from well north of Cairns to Lizard Island, about 160 kilometres up the track.

And working their way north, fishing the Ribbons as they went, required a decent-sized live-aboard boat – something big enough to accommodate a cook, anglers and crew. As most of the fishing boats were small, quick and more manoeuvrable, motherships which could take up to three boats and their occupants at a time were built.

They would meander up the coast inside the reef, and have dinner and a cold drink waiting for the day-boats at the end of a hard day's fishing.

Soon it became impractical to go back to Cairns at all. Day-boats would go out and stay out for three months at a time, living off and refuelling from the motherships and flying their anglers out by float plane – yet another business that was created to cater to the demands of the ever-increasing marlin fleet.

My home for the 10 days was the 120 foot *Achilles II*, the largest mothership in the fleet, with a replacement value of around $12 million. Sitting like a satellite city inside the No. 5 Ribbon Reef, it made our 40 foot day-boat, *Reel Affair*, look like a dingy. Still, at upwards of $2000 a day for each boat, and up to three boats at a time, you would expect the ultimate. We were the only boat living on it at the time, so we had the *Achilles II* and its doting crew all to ourselves.

As I arrived by float plane, Brazakka was waiting on the back of *Achilles II* to meet me.

'Say hello to Big Bill from Texas,' he said as he introduced us. Bill was a giant of a man, with shoulders like a padded-up gridiron player.

'How y'all doin'?' he grinned as he plonked his mitt around mine and shook it until my whole body ached. 'Brazakka tells me you're a gonna gaff that big fish for me. It don't worry ya none, does it? Killin' one of 'em, ah mean?'

'No, not at all,' I replied. 'That's what I'm here for.'

'Good,' he exclaimed. 'Me and my darlin' Connie have been comin' down here these past five years and I reckon it's time for me to take one big 'un.'

So off we went – no time to unpack. I just loaded my gear into my cabin and we took off fishing. Under normal circumstances I would be disappointed to go home after a day's fishing. But getting back to the *Achilles* at night was a real treat – a chilled beer, fabulous food and a chat about the day's events. And there was plenty to talk about. The first couple of days were good, with a few fish up to 400 pounds released. The fourth day was one of the best fishing days of my life. We were fishing

Mark, the deckie, with an average-sized bait for the giant Cairns black marlin.

off the No. 10 Ribbon and the bite was hot. We got 10 fish up, six of them bit, and we hooked up and released four. The biggest was around 800 pounds – a whopper by my standards, but only a tiddler compared with what was to come.

It was on the fifth day that Mrs Huge appeared behind the baits. She was lit up like a fire cracker, pectorals a stark white and her barrel torso a myriad of fluorescent blue and white bars, something that they do when they are about to eat or mate. Brazakka turned the boat out of the sun so he could get a better look at the fish.

'Big bastard,' he mumbled. That's about as excited as he got. He normally loves a chat, but not when the bite's on.

She took the bait and Brazakka gunned the boat ahead and hooked up. *Reel Affair* went nose first into the 5 metre swell with the huge marlin peeling off the 130 pound line against 60 pounds of clutch pressure as if it was a roll of toilet paper. Big Bill had his work cut out just getting the rod from the gunwale to the chair unaided.

At last he was settled and Mark, the deckie, buckled him up to the harness. Only now did I see why the big Southerner's angling ability was

It was hard to imagine that anything that big could get itself out of the water.

held in such high esteem. His powerful legs and back combined to put pressure against the fish and gain line at every opportunity. But as much as the Texan took, the big fish took it back.

The acrobatics were spectacular. How anything that big could propel itself clear of the water was beyond me. 'How big?' I asked Brazakka. 'Between thirteen and fourteen hundred,' he growled, and he'd know.

I stayed out of the way on the flying bridge. My gaffs were ready in the cockpit, secured to the stem of the fighting chair. Soon I would have to earn my keep.

And so the fight continued; fortunately, it was on or near the surface, away from the sharks. Then she didn't jump any more. She just bogged down into the current about 20 metres below the surface, with Brazakka full speed in reverse after her.

Two hours later, Big Bill was holding up pretty well. He could still manage a huge grin. 'This is the hardest fish I ever fought,' he said. 'She just don't wanna die.'

After two and a half hours, it was time. The trace was up and Mark took a wrap in his heavily gloved hands and lifted the mammoth fish towards the boat. I was beside him, with my gaff ready. 'Don't choke,' he said. 'Just a neat shot in the shoulder.'

By now all 5 metres of the giant fish was coming. I was mesmerised by the sheer size of her as her head – with a beak like a baseball bat and an eye the size of a bread and butter plate – broke the surface in an attempt to leap about 5 metres away from the boat.

Until my dying breath I will never forget the look of defiance and fear in her giant eye. My reflection seemed to disappear deep into it as I prepared to kill her. She was tired from the fight. Brazakka inched the boat back and Mark took bigger wraps on the trace. It was almost time for the kill.

I readied my gaff. Another few centimetres and I would impale her and she would die. So close now.

The water was pouring into the cockpit as we reversed into the sea. Now she was alongside, perfectly positioned for me to perform my duty. I steadied …

'No,' called the big Texan. 'Cut her loose.'

'What the fuck …' I yelled.

'Don't argue,' he commanded. 'Let her go.'

Mark cut the wire and the huge fish swam off into the abyss. I was dumbfounded. I turned to the big Texan, who was smiling. Nothing was said. It wasn't necessary.

I looked up at the skipper and he was smiling too.

The Deaf Snapper

*Fishing and villains seem to go hand in hand. Legend
has it that from time to time fishing boats are used to
pick up drug hauls out at sea or dispose of bodies. Mafia
Godfather John Gotti operated out of New Jersey's
Bergen Hunt and Fish Club. There's usually a marlin
or a sailfish on the wall in a movie gangster's office.
And Al Capone loved to fish when he was in Florida.
This is a gangster fishing story.*

Back in the 1960s, when Sir Robert Askin ruled the Sydney
underworld from Parliament House, a 'made man' of the Mafia,
Don Georgio Spilotro, lorded over his flourishing starting price
gambling empire with a fist of tungsten and a smoking gun.

This was long before the days of the TAB – the only way to get a bet
on without going to the racecourse was through an illegal SP bookie,
and they were about as hard to find as bikinis on Bondi Beach.

In one way or another, Don Georgio controlled the vast percentage of the
SPs, as he had the Premier's ear and saw to it that for a weekly
consideration the police turned a blind eye to his bookies, who operated out
of hotels, clubs and anywhere else the punter was likely to want to get set.

And they bet on anything … the gallops, trots, dogs … even the 18 footer sailing races on Sydney Harbour.

Don Georgio was the most frightening human being I have ever laid eyes on. Tall and lean, athletically fit, immaculately groomed and with an eye as black as a November nor'-wester, Don Georgio looked considerably younger than his 50 years. He also sported a long, jagged scar that ran from just beneath his left eye, over which he wore a black eye-patch, to the corner of his mouth.

He had the swarthy, handsome, Ricardo Montalban, European-type looks that the women of the day swooned over.

Legend had it that the young Georgio Spilotro picked up his facial souvenir some 25 years earlier in a knife fight – to the death – with Mick the Turk over control of Sydney's inner-city brothels.

The Turk was all over him, apparently, and with blood pouring from his punctured eyeball, Georgio took one last desperate lunge and slit the Turk's throat from ear to ear. He then sliced off his enemy's ears as souvenirs and pissed in the gaping throat wound.

From that day on, no one fucked with Georgio Spilotro or his team of hoods, and as he graduated from running whorehouses to the much more respectable business of SP gambling, his legend grew, and he was bestowed the honour of being titled Don Georgio by his peers.

Don Georgio wore his scar and eye-patch as a badge of honour.

Stories of his methods of collecting from the unfortunates who had got in too deep or had taken the knock were told throughout the Sydney underworld.

His favourite method was to have his chief executioner, Chiller, hang a victim on a meat hook in the back of a refrigerated meat truck until the poor bastard either came good with the money or froze to death.

The Don had two favourite recreations. One was hooning around Sydney Harbour in the summer months with his boat full of colourful characters, drinking French champagne, snorting cocaine and copulating with an endless supply of topless beauties who queued up at the wharf in the hope that they may get invited out for a lavish day of sin and lust on the harbour.

But his real passion was fishing Sydney's offshore reefs for bottom species such as snapper and kingfish. However, he never seemed to have much luck.

The Don had started out his boating career with a modest 7.5 metre Bertram and had worked his way up slowly through the years to his beloved 15 metre Chris Craft *Georgie Boy*.

Like most men from humble beginnings, he adored his magnificent toy with a passion and kept it in mint condition.

Back in those days I fished with Keith Whitehead on his 11 metre Bertram, *Splashdown*, and every time we came back from fishing off Sydney Heads with a marlin or a shark dragging off the back of the boat and we passed the Don and his team on the harbour, Keith would wave to him as he stood in the cockpit, tanned and fit, cigar in one hand, champagne flute in the other and a dozen topless to-die-for babes hanging off him and his cronies.

'How do you catch those things?' he asked Keith, pointing at the fish hanging off the back of the boat and ogling the big snapper we held up. 'I've been out there this morning and I caught nothin'. How come you bastards are so smart?'

Keith would wave back and say, 'It's the gear, Don Georgio. You've gotta have the right equipment. If you decked your boat out for fishing you'd catch more fish. It's as simple as that.'

Don Georgio's favourite of all of the girls at the time was a showgirl named Stella, who was about as close to a permanent girlfriend as he would ever allow. Stella was a party girl who looked for all the world like Marilyn Monroe, but with black hair.

The Don used to take Stella out fishing with him, and her giant boobs and wiggling butt drove the other blokes on the boat nuts. Stella spent half her time pampering the boss and the other half getting her stiletto heels out of the gaps in the planks along the marina.

At the time, Keith Whitehead had the agency for Chris Craft boats. He had sold Don Georgio *Georgie Boy* in exchange for a big bag of cash. Keith knew that the Don had a lot of 'black' money to play with, spoils of his illegal gambling operations, and he also knew that the Don was a sucker for buying things.

Naturally, the more equipment Keith could sell Don Georgio for his boat, the more commission he earned.

Keith was in the process of outfitting an identical boat to *Georgie Boy* for a well-known racing car driver, so every time he bought a new toy for the other boat he would make a point of driving the boat under Don Georgio's nose, displaying the new gear.

The gamefishing chair was the best in the world, and cost around ten grand. It looked like the barber's chair that Albert Anastasia was murdered in; a good selling point, no doubt.

When the Don cast his black eyes over that heavily chromed work of art he was entranced.

'What's that fuckin' thing?' he asked, pointing at the chair. 'Why don't I have one of them?'

'That's a fighting chair, Don Georgio. For sitting in and fighting big fish. It's the best in the world,' Whitehead replied. 'Looks good on that rig doesn't it? You're mad if you don't put one on *Georgie Boy*. You'll look great in it. And besides, it'll help you catch more fish.'

The beautiful thing was that Don Georgio never asked the price of anything. All he wanted to do was catch more fish.

'Then you'd better get me one of those things,' he'd say.

A week later Keith paraded past with the latest pair of pronged outrigger poles fitted to the sides of the other boat.

'What's those things?' the Don pointed.

'Aluminium six-prongers,' Whitehead explained. 'You can troll six marlin baits at once. They're guaranteed to catch you fish.'

No one on Don Georgio's boat knew how to rig a marlin bait, let alone troll six at once, but the poles made the boat look great, so the Boss would have to have a pair.

'Get those poles too, then,' he demanded.

Within a few days the poles were fitted to *Georgie Boy* – and they looked great.

After six months *Georgie Boy* looked like an ocean-going ship's chandlery.

Three ship-to-shore radios, radar, depth sounders, satellite navigation, quadraphonic stereo … the works. It had every piece of equipment money could buy.

And so, week after week, Whitehead would enquire as he passed *Georgie Boy* back in its berth at the marina after a morning's fishing: 'How'd you go today, Don Georgio? Did you catch any fish?'

Don Georgio's reply was standard. He would scowl at Whitehead. 'No stinkin' fish again today,' he would grumble. 'I spend a hundred grand on the best boat gear with you, and still I can't catch fuckin' fish. What's goin' wrong?'

This went on for months. One Saturday afternoon, as *Georgie Boy* had just been tied up in its pen fresh back from a day's fishing, Whitehead didn't even bother to ask how they went; instead he offered the Don some advice.

'I think I've worked out why you never catch any fish, Don Georgio,' he said.

The Don was in the barber's chair sipping from a champagne flute and sucking on a White Owl cigar. Chiller had just tied off the boat and was about to cut into his first tinny. Stella was hovering, with her giant tits hanging out, and an assortment of the Don's cronies were lurking about getting drinks.

They all pricked up their ears to listen to the old master.

'What's the first thing you do when you moor up at Long Reef?' Whitehead asked. 'In fact, don't even bother answering. I know, you turn all the toys on at once, don't you?'

'Of course I do,' the Don replied. 'What's the use of the gear if I'm not gonna use it?'

'It's the noise,' replied Whitehead

'What do you mean it's the noise?'

'Well, you've got the stereos going at nine million decibels and the generator at full bore to run the air conditioning, right? And you know how Chiller likes to watch the radar beacon going round and round. Then there's the echo sounders, the two-way radios and the Randwick Races – all going at a million miles an hour.

'And Stella's high heels on the deck don't help. Believe me, Don Georgio. I reckon I've worked out why you don't catch any fish. It's the noise.'

'What do you mean it's the noise?' The Don still couldn't understand what Whitehead was saying and was getting the shits.

'Let me explain,' Whitehead continued. 'All that racket that you make in the boat goes straight through the hull and bounces off the reef, scaring the shit out of the fish. They all piss off. It's as simple as that. It's the noise – that's why you don't catch any fish.'

The Don looked at his motley crew in amazement.

'Well I'll be!' he exclaimed. 'So that's what's been goin' wrong. You smart bastard! Why didn't someone tell me that? You're one very clever bastard, you know that?'

Whitehead kept a straight face.

With that the Don got up from the barber's chair and walked over to the coffin-sized Esky at the back of the boat. He opened the lid. It was chock-a-block with giant snapper. Whitehead's eyes nearly fell out of his head.

'OK, Mr Boat Dealer, you're so fuckin' smart,' Don Georgio said, holding up two whoppers. 'Now I suppose you're gonna tell me that these fuckin' beauties are all deaf!'

The crew cracked up.

You see, unbeknownst to Keith, Don Georgio had recruited the services of the legendary Sydney Harbour boatman-cum-fisherman Dicey Frankman, and following Dicey's directions and knowledge of the moon, tides and currents, they had been filling the boat with fish every time they went out. Even Stella, Chiller and all the hangers-on got to catch a fish. The Don was hooked, and from that day on he lived for fishing. And Dicey knew where to find 'em.

He showered Dicey with gifts and told him that if Dicey ever fished with anyone else he'd have the poor bastard's boat blown out of the water and he'd piss down the owner's throat after he'd slit it. And yes, Dicey *had* heard the legendary story, so he saw to it that he was available whenever the Don needed him.

Unfortunately, Dicey got horribly pissed one night and fell off the end of the Double Bay marina. When the cops found him two days later – in Rose Bay, covered in prawns and very deceased – the Don was distraught.

'You think I'm gonna rub out the guy who catches me all the fish?' he explained to the cops who, naturally enough, considered him a prime suspect.

But we all knew it was an accident. The Don loved Dicey, and the fact was that without him he couldn't catch any fish.

No matter what he offered, Don Georgio couldn't get anyone else to fish with him. It seemed the whole waterfront had heard the stories about the Don's unusual urinary habits.

Don Georgio eventually gave up fishing, and as the newly introduced TAB started to take a giant slice out of his illegal gambling, he ventured into more sinister activities.

Often we would see the magnificent *Georgie Boy* moored up in some secluded bay on Sydney Harbour with a bunch of bad-looking dudes on board. Keith gave Don Georgio a wide berth – he said the Don was mixed up in heavy drugs these days and it was only a matter of time before something went wrong.

And it did. One day Don Georgio disappeared off the face of the planet. But we all figured that his love of fishing wasn't all in vain. According to Mob folklore, Don Georgio now sleeps with his beloved fishes.

Those Magnificently Mad Makos

Of all of the critters that swim, there is nothing
more dangerous or maniacal than the mako shark.
If they were humans they would spend their entire
lives in mental institutions. Everything you read
about them is true. I doubt that anyone could have a
vivid enough imagination to make up the bizarre
nature of a mako.

W hen a 3 metre 200 kilogram mako shark tried to eat Gordon Dunlop's 6 metre fibreglass fishing boat about 10 kilometres off Sydney and then attempted to jump into it, it was yet another chapter in a long and bizarre series of incidents involving mako sharks.

But all you once-a-year anglers out there needn't worry. The chances of you ever getting bitten, let alone eaten, by a mako are pretty remote unless you venture out into the very deep waters where the manic mako, aka the blue pointer, rules the currents. It fears nothing except perhaps bigger and crazier makos.

In fact, if a mako did eat you, your death would not be in vain – you would go down in history as the first recorded victim of a mako shark in Australian waters. Except, of course, for the folk who may have been

frightened to death by them or come very close. And there's no shortage of them. Gordon is now on the end of a very long list.

Yes, makos are homicidal maniacs. Growing to 750 kilograms, built like guided missiles with magnificent steely silver-blue backs, snow-white undercarriages and eyes that are as black as a mother-in-law's curse that follow your every move from the water, mako sharks are Mother Nature's ultimate killing machines.

But man-eaters? No. Certainly not to my knowledge anyway. But the curator of the Taronga Zoo Aquarium, John West (no, I'm not having you on), who also records shark attacks in Australian waters, says differently.

'The mako, a close cousin of the great white shark, is a known man-killer in some parts of the world, but there have been no confirmed attacks in Australia,' John said in an interview. 'But shark experts rate them as potentially dangerous.'

Potentially dangerous? That would have to be the greatest under-statement since Greg Norman gave up surfing and said, 'I might take up golf. I think I could be good at it.' Potentially dangerous? Really? A shark that has been known to jump into boats, terrorise the living daylights out of the occupants and then jump out again is *potentially* dangerous? A shark that on dozens of occasions has been known to grab the propeller or leg of an outboard motor in its crockery-encrusted gob-hole and then shake the motor and boat while the poor wretches on board go white with fear in a real-life scene that would make *Jaws* look like *Here's Humphrey* is potentially dangerous?

No, makos aren't potentially dangerous ... they are *definitely*

The business end of a giant mako. It's little wonder they almost frighten people to death.

dangerous. I've been telling stories about the antics of mako sharks for nigh on 30 years now, and I'll tell more about them in a minute, but first let me quote a couple of paragraphs from Gordon about his experience with that horrible critter he encountered while he was berleying and drifting for yellowfin tuna.

'It appeared in the berley and circled the boat before slamming into it a number of times, smashing teeth as it savaged the two outboard motors and part of the gunwale,' Gordon said. 'It left giant gouges in the metal of the main 140 horsepower motor. But things really got interesting when it tried to get into the boat. It came in over the stern and got so close to me I could have poked it in the eye.'

Dodging to avoid the snapping jaws, Gordon hit the mako over the head with a length of wood normally used to stun tuna. It eventually slithered back into the water and swam off, 'shaking its head in the air as if it was convulsing'. Eventually it recovered fully and swam away, much to the relief of Gordon and his crew.

John West believes that this mako's aggressive behaviour was caused by the pilchards that the fishermen were throwing over the side to attract

This little mako seemed passive enough after it jumped into a boat and terrified the occupants. It was quickly thrown back in.

24

tuna, some run-off blood from the bait tank, and electromagnetic fields around the outboard motor – the mako is extremely sensitive to these because they resemble ones produced by the heart muscles of potential prey.

Hmm. That's all very well, but having been nearly killed by makos on more than one occasion, I have a different theory. The pilchards, blood and electromagnetic field all add up, but what John has omitted to tell us is that during late August, September and October, the mako sharks gather off the east coast of Australia, particularly off Sydney, to mate. That's right, to mate.

Yeah, I know the old gag: 'How do they do it? Very carefully.' But this is no laughing matter, particularly for the makos. There are some pretty cranky old makos out there this time of the year, and to make it worse, there are not enough lady makos to go round, so to speak, so they get even crankier, particularly if they happen to find a mate and someone tries to take her away, or even worse, succeeds in taking her away.

Every year about this time I used to go mako shark fishing off Sydney Heads, and what we saw out there was so pathetic that if it weren't so serious (to the sharks) it would have been hilarious – which, to us, it was.

Doey-eyed makos lolling around on the surface, too love-sick to take a bait or care about anything but a bit of lust. And then there are the poor buggers with giant gouges out of them either from the love-making process – which is extremely aggressive – or from fending off the advances of would-be suitors.

And then there are the ones who appeared to have missed out altogether. They scurry about all over the joint, really pissed off, ravenously attacking our baits. Once hooked, they jump all over the ocean. Actually, they don't actually jump; they launch themselves from the water like Patriot missiles, reaching heights of 10 metres or more.

It is a style unique to the mako, no matter where or what time of the year you hook them, and it is both breathtaking and terrifying to watch. And yes, they have landed in boats. And yes, more times than once, when a mako has landed in a boat the occupants have been known to jump out.

Like the time in New Zealand a few years back when a whopper mako jumped into a gamefishing boat. A couple of the anglers jumped over the side while another two fled to the saloon of the boat, locked the door and waited while the mako kicked the game chair, rods and reels into the next postcode.

Only after the fish had exhausted itself did the fishermen gingerly emerge from the saloon. They clubbed it to death with a fire extinguisher and then helped their mates back on board. Is it any wonder they are referred to in fishing circles as 'blue dynamite with a short fuse'?

But the classic story of them all happened off Sydney Heads back in the 1970s. A lone angler in his 12 metre cabin cruiser was moored up fishing for snapper on the bottom and for sharks on the surface with a floating bait. The shark bait went off, and as he picked up the rod and reel and set the hook he was amazed to see a huge mako shark, around 350 kilograms, jump clear of the water then land on his line and break it.

Terrified by the size of the mako and aware that he would have no chance of catching it by himself, he put the shark gear away and concentrated on his snapper fishing. But the mako had other ideas. It charged the tuck of the boat a couple of times before making a giant leap, propelling itself into the cockpit, where it went berserk and smashed, bit and kicked the shit out of everything in sight.

Our hero fled to the flying bridge. He got out an old .303 rifle from beneath the bench seat and blazed away at the beast that was reducing his beautiful boat to a splintered, blood- and foam-soaked mess. But unfortunately for him, every shot missed the shark and instead went straight through the deck and into the engines or through the bottom of the boat.

The mako jumped over the side and circled the boat as the angler managed to get one engine going, cut the anchor rope and head for home, with water pouring in from everywhere. In answer to his mayday call, the water police met him halfway and towed him back through the Heads. Only then did the mako stop following the boat and head back out to sea.

And that's a true story. They tell me that ever since that day the poor bastard won't even drink water with his Scotch, let alone ever go back out fishing in it.

Skidmarks and The Judge

There is little doubt that cheating goes on in fishing competitions, but the characters in this true story were so blatant about it that to this day no one knows how they got away with it. The fact that two dopes with only half a brain between them could devise such a scheme is the most amazing part.

The State Fishing Titles were the ultimate event in club fishing championships, and to win any one of the major categories meant fishing immortality. This was the event where superstars were born, and living legends in the fishing world such as Clem 'Stumps' Hall and 'Three Fingers' (Sid White) came into being.

Legend has it that Stumps was blitzing the trevally and tailor at the bottom of a 100 metre cliff in horrendous conditions when he was swept into the drink by a huge wave. He hung on to a rock for almost 10 hours before someone spotted him. A rescue helicopter arrived just in time to pluck him out.

But they didn't arrive in time to save a few of his fingers, which were cut off at the stumps by the razor-sharp barnacle and oyster shells on the rock he was hanging on to. Hence the nickname.

But even after this near-death experience – and being relieved of a few of his digits – Stumps' only concern was winning the coveted Champion Angler trophy, so he scaled back down the face of the cliff in a force 10 gale, recovered his fish and had them back at the weigh-in just in time to take out top honours.

So extraordinary was his achievement that they named the bar at the club after him, an honour beyond the wildest dreams of any club angler.

Three Fingers wasn't so fortunate. His lifelong ambition was to catch the heaviest fish of the Titles, and he had prepared his plan of attack a long time in advance. A year or so before the event, he coaxed a 10 kilogram blue groper out of its cave on a secluded headland by sitting on the rocks for days on end throwing tiny morsels to it in an effort to befriend it. He returned to the same spot without fail every day, always with tasty offerings, and within six months he had the groper – which he had christened 'Bluey' and which by now weighed about 40 kilograms – almost eating out of his hand.

By a week before the Titles, the groper would do anything that Sid commanded as long as he supplied more food – it was now grossly obese, having ballooned out to about 75 kilograms.

Sid's plan was simple. On the first day of the Titles he visited the groper and hand-fed it a whole 5 kilogram snapper from the markets. However, this snapper had a hook in it. The hook was attached to a 1000 kilogram breaking strain trace, which in turn was connected to 500 kilogram main line and a shark rod and one of those huge old-fashioned revolving drum reels with protruding handles and no anti-reverse. Most certainly not the kind of gear to be catching gargantuan groper with, but then Sid wasn't exactly brain surgeon material.

Once the unsuspecting groper had taken the snapper, Sid snuck off to a makeshift fighting chair he had built out of rocks about 20 metres from the water's edge and settled in to take up the slack line and drag the groper out of the water.

The theory was that one of two things would happen. He would catch the fish before it was aware of what was going on or it would feel the

hook, take off and more than likely break the line. He hadn't counted on a third alternative.

He slowly retrieved the slack line, and as soon as he felt some pressure he leaned back into the shark rod with all his might to set the hook. That's when his theories of what would happen jumped out of the window. He didn't catch the groper and the line didn't break. Instead, the giant fishing reel handles revolved backwards in a blur as the huge fish felt the resistance of the line, realised that something was drastically wrong and headed back to its cave at a million miles an hour, dragging with it the rod and reel and a couple of Sid's fingers that had been unlucky enough to be in the way.

Even though he didn't win the Biggest Fish trophy, Sid gained legendary status with that little episode, and it's obvious that he would rather hear the story about himself told over and over again than have his fingers back.

Which leads me to the tale of Skidmarks and The Judge and how they won the famed Doubles Event – the most coveted trophy of them all. The rules of the State Titles were simple: the prize was for total weight. There were no boundaries and no line classes. Just catch-and-kill fishing.

The only hard and fast rule was that berleying before the event was not allowed; it would give the berleyers an unfair advantage in that the fish would be waiting to be caught come competition time. Outside that it was open slather.

Skidmarks and The Judge were a couple of wharfies who were desperate for a little fame and recognition, and they figured that the only way they could do it was through fishing. Skidmarks got his nickname because he was always going to 'follow through' on something that was brought up at a trade union meeting at which he was a delegate. 'Leave it with me. I'll follow through on it,' was Skidmark's trademark promise. He never did.

They called his mate The Judge because he spent all his time sitting on a case.

For their devious scheme they co-opted the services of 'Mirrors' ('I'll look into it for you') Marsden, another wharfie, who just happened to live next door to the Hearty Host pie factory and through a hole in the fence had access to the reject pie bin. And believe me, there were plenty of rejects.

Every night for three months before the State Titles they loaded up Mirrors' ute with reject gravy-dripping pies and dumped them off the cliffs at the Devil's Gorge, a fishing spot that had been abandoned years earlier because it was too dangerous. No one ever went there any more.

It took a couple of days for the first fish to show up, but as soon as the word got out that there was a free feed on every night, every fish within a hundred kilometres, including marlin, sharks and tuna, was there with its mouth open. Come the day of the State Titles, the Devil's Gorge was wall-to-wall fish – they outnumbered the pies by about ten to one.

With the help of Mirrors (who wasn't even entered in the event), they filled the ute in no time, took it to the weigh-in, emptied it and returned for more. That pair of cheats cleaned up just about everything, including the coveted Doubles Event. They got biggest fish of most species, winning team and a host of other cash and prizes.

Everyone smelled a rat, because that pair were so stupid that they had trouble catching a bus, let alone a couple of truckloads of fish. But there wasn't a darn thing anyone could do about it.

When the truth eventually came out – they mouthed off about their cunning scheme one night when they were pissed – I did recall looking at their ute outside the club on presentation night and wondering why there were a hundred cats licking out the back of the ute and a dozen dogs licking the chassis.

I remember thinking, 'That's funny. Dogs don't like fish.'

Flies, like Martinis,
Should Be Dry

*Have you ever wondered why the folk who fly-fish are
generally regarded as a bunch of snobs by the bluewater
brigade? It's probably because a vast percentage of them
are. And lots of them make no bones about their upper-
class pastime and its ancestry.*

Until recent years, I had always reckoned that most of the fly-
fishing fraternity were a bunch of elitist snobs. To my mind
they try to give the impression that they are better than
anyone else and that their chosen form of fishing is much more difficult
than all the other forms of angling put together.

The 'gentleman's sport', I think they call it. Something that could be
likened to fox-hunting, rugby and rowing. Strictly for the old school tie
brigade.

But just because I think like that doesn't mean I'm right. Far from it.
Lots of blokes I know these days who go fly-fishing certainly wouldn't
fit into that category.

I'm sure famous anglers such as Andrew Ettingshausen, Steve
Starling, Bushy, Garry McDonald and Charles Wooley wouldn't like to
be classed as toffs, and they are all fanatical fly-fishers. And, as blokes,

you couldn't meet a more down-to-earth bunch. There's certainly no old school tie about any of them.

Before we saw Aussies fly-fishing on the telly, the only time we would see it done was on some show from England with Algernon Boring-Poof in his gingham shirt and Eton tie blurting on about mayfly this and muddler-minnow that and casting into a stream in the shadows of a 500-year-old castle owned by Lord Marmaduke Shagnasty. Groan.

But nowadays I can assure you that there are plenty of ordinary blokes and women out there getting into fly-fishing without all the pomp and crap that used to go with it. I doubt you would find Charlie or ET wandering around a lake or a mountain stream sporting a cravat and a velvet jacket with leather elbows.

And if some of the fellows casting handmade artificial enticements at the rainbows and browns these days aren't wearing that old traditional clobber, does it mean that one of the oldest forms of angling is now conforming to today's standards?

What a ghastly suggestion, old boy. Heaven forbid!

Even with today's fly-fishers being a little less rigid, why do I always associate them with pomp, ancient ports and whiskeys and old money? I've asked myself this question often. But why would I bother wasting my time thinking about the trouties anyway?

It all has to do with my job as a fishing writer – fly-fishing is becoming more and more a part of what I write about, so I might as well come to terms with the diggers who do it.

Maybe it's the tradition of dry fly-fishing that makes me think it's only for the snooty few. The fact that it dates back to the late 18th century and that it was the favoured pastime of kings of England, lords and knights of the realm – it's definitely a sport that is as historical as it is recreational.

I think that to some, the trout is only a minuscule part of the art of fly-fishing. For the would-bes, who are, fortunately, a dying breed, I suspect the sport is more about dressage, social status and class values.

And I think that the majority of those old duffers who fly-fish are in it more for the bullshit value than for anything else. Most of them are pompous whiskey-swilling old farts who get their kicks sitting around in a gentlemen's club pissing in each other's ears about the one that got away.

When it comes to snobbery, some of the exclusive fly-fishermen's clubs in Tasmania take the cake. Their members refer to themselves as 'purists' – they would never dream of using a bait or lure. They only use dry flies, the ones that float on the top; they never use those 'vulgar' wet flies that go under the water and therefore are the next best thing to bait.

They wear all the top clobber. Checked shirts and tartan ties. Leather-elbowed tweed jackets with matching hats covered in a variety of flies. Some of them

To fish the dry fly, the angler must wear the right gear – these days, it is nothing like what their fishing ancestors used to prance around in.

stomp through the undergrowth in 'plus fours' and brogue shoes, with the inevitable hip flask and briar pipe.

A Tasmanian fly-fishing mate of mine – who prefers to remain nameless for fear of reprisals – tells of two members of a Tassie 'purists' club who were sprung bait-fishing for trout. It was a dull, overcast day and the trout weren't rising. They had found a couple of their great-grandchildren's spinning rods in the boot of the Rover, so they baited them up with witchetty grubs for a bit of fun.

But they were sprung by one of the members hiding behind a nearby tree. I wouldn't even attempt to guess what he was doing there.

The pair were hauled before the committee and members at a special meeting, and in true British court-martial tradition were found guilty of the most heinous of crimes – attempting to catch trout on bait.

They were made to stand in front of everyone while the president stripped their tweed hats off, broke their fly rods over his knee and sent them off into the night, banished for life, never to be seen again. Bloody good show, old chap. That'll teach them not to try to enjoy themselves. How dare they!

Every time my mate tells me that story I picture them as a club full of old goats, all of whom look like the major out of *Fawlty Towers*. My nameless mate swears blind that it's a true story, and he has many more instances just like it to prove that tradition is alive and well on the Apple Isle.

And my mate would know. After all, he's a true-blue Taswegian and proud of it, though he admits that some of the trouties go a tiny bit over the top.

But he is quick to add that you haven't lived until you've caught a trout on a dry (floating) fly.

So why is it that everyone associates dry fly-fishing for trout with the landed gentry and other assorted toffs? I asked my wife, who knows as much about fly-fishing as I know about wildebeest breeding, and even she said that she always thought of fly-fishers as a bunch of snobs.

Releasing a Tasmanian brown trout caught, of course old chap, on the dry fly.

There was only one way to find out. I rang my friend John Turnbull in Canberra. John is one of Australia's foremost authorities on trout, and has spent a lifetime writing articles and books about them, catching them and studying them. If anyone would know, it would be the old master himself.

'Wet fly-fishing goes back 2000 years,' John told me. 'The Roman historian Marcus Aurelius, who was a sort of travelling journalist of the times, described flies that are the equivalent of the Red Hackle fly which is still in use today. The Macedonians were fishing with flies about 260 AD. But these were all wet flies. The dry fly was invented around the 1880s, after someone invented the rods to cast them with.

'The best fishing spots were in the south of England and France, in chalk streams. These streams were extremely fertile, as the dissolving nutrients would percolate through the chalk, providing the lush weed growth that is the home of the insects that are the main food source of the trout. As these trout loved a feed of hatching insects, they often rose to feed on the surface. When they did, the only way to catch them was with a dry fly.

'And where did we find these streams?' John continued. 'On the vast country estates of the privileged, of course. So when the old farts and their entourages of whores tired of gorging, boozing, lusting and playing badminton and croquet, they wandered down to the stream in their silks and wigs and, under instructions from the estate fishing master, endeavoured to catch a trout while they sipped their vintage Dom Perignon.

'That's where the aristocracy got involved; and that's the way it is with some people even to this day.

'But even in those bygone times,' John Turnbull added, 'the pretenders got to be somebody marvellous just by getting into dry fly-fishing. Amazing, but true. The silliest thing about this kerfuffle is the fact that trout are one of the easiest fish in the world to catch on the dry fly.'

Need I say more?

Toady's Revenge

This story is the reason why I believe that if you are cruel to animals, or for that matter, any living thing, it will come back on you one day. I would ask every parent to encourage their children to read this story, to make them aware of the dangers that lie ahead for young people who are cruel to harmless animals.

When I was a kid growing up in Perth, my mates and I tried to commit genocide on a loathsome creature called the 'blowie'. Not the blowfly – the blowfish. That's what we called them over there. No matter where we fished, sooner or later the blowies would turn up in their millions and take over. And they were not a pretty sight.

Growing to about 30 centimetres long, blowies were brown along the back with a snow-white underbelly that puffed up like a prickly balloon when they were caught; they had big bulging bug eyes like a cane toad and a pair of square teeth that would make Goofy look gormless.

To say the least, they were bloody pests, and once they showed up we had to pack up and leave because the chance of catching anything else was pretty remote. They were useless for anything: no good as bait, and we read regularly in the papers how people had died or at least got very

36

sick from eating them. And so, with the Department of Fisheries' full approval, we took it upon ourselves to rid Perth's waterways of this menace.

We killed every one that we caught. And savage little bastards that we were, we devised the most horrific methods of dispatch imaginable. We stabbed them, threw them under cars on the Canning Bridge, teed off using them as golf balls, left them to die in agony in the hot sun, stuck crackers up their arses and lit them, extracted their teeth while they were still alive and let them go with their entrails hanging out so the other blowies could eat them alive.

My father was appalled at the carnage. 'Let me tell you a little story about life,' he said to me as he sat me down and tried to explain to me how whatever we do always comes back to us in some form or another. He called it 'karma'. 'When I was a young boy living on a farm,' he said, 'there was a billygoat living in the paddock next door. The poor old billygoat had never done anything to me, but I used to chuck rocks at it all the time. I never hit it, and it was smart enough to stay out of range. After a while the grass close to the fence grew long and rich, because the billygoat never came close enough to eat it for fear of being hit with a rock.

'Then I stayed away for awhile, and sure enough, the goat started to graze closer and closer to the fence, gaining more and more bravado as each day passed. So one day when it was happily munching away just on the other side of the fence, I snuck up and threw a full house brick at it. I hit it square between the eyes. The poor old goat went down and didn't move. I was mortified. I had no idea that I could kill it. I just wanted to have some fun with it, and now it was stone dead. My father thrashed me to within an inch of my life. And as if that wasn't bad enough, he made a chilling prediction that has lived with me all my life.

'He said that no matter where I went or whatever I did, that goat would haunt me for the rest of my days. "It may not be in the shape of a goat," he said. "It could be a future boss, a bad motor car or just a bad circumstance in life. But no matter what, every time something rotten happens, you can bet your life that if you close your eyes tight enough, you'll see that goat looking up at you and laughing its head off."

'And it was true. All my life, whenever something has gone wrong, or bad unforeseen circumstances have occurred, that goat has flashed across my consciousness, and when I closed my eyes, there it was, having a laugh at my expense. Mind you, what you are doing to those unfortunate blowies is nowhere near as bad as what I did to that poor old goat, because the blowies are toxic pests, but you can bet your life that somewhere, sometime, there will be an even up. Life's like that.'

I discarded what my wise old dad had told me as a load of crap, and went about devising new horrendous methods of disposing of the blowies. We set fire to them, skinned them alive and gouged their eyes out. So much for 'karma'. I told my mates what Dad had said, and after that they would stab the blowies repeatedly and yell out 'karma, karma, karma' while they were doing it. We were horrid little beasts.

In my late teens I moved to Sydney and blowies became a thing of the past, because they are very rare around the east coast. Soon I had forgotten about them altogether as I pursued a blowie-less fishing career around the stunning rock ledges, undersea mountains and warm ocean currents that combine to make the eastern seaboard of Australia one of the fishiest places on Earth. In the late 1960s I started writing feature fishing stories for national magazines and a weekly column in the local eastern suburbs newspaper. In 1972 I opened a fishing tackle shop in Bondi Junction, and it became the centre of fishing activity in the district. I had set myself up as the local expert, which, in hindsight, left me wide open for any form of practical joke. After all, experts are supposed to be invincible, aren't they?

So when my mate Thommo asked me to partner him in the local Fishing Derby, which offered cash prizes for the heaviest of *any* species weighed, I jumped at the chance. Thommo was a hotshot angler and knew Sydney Harbour and the close offshore reefs backwards. If we couldn't take out a few prizes, no one could. We started red-hot favourites.

But it just wasn't my day. We fished Long Reef, about 6 kilometres off Sydney Heads, in Thommo's 9 metre boat. Just before daylight he caught a jewie that must have weighed about 15 kilograms, and as the

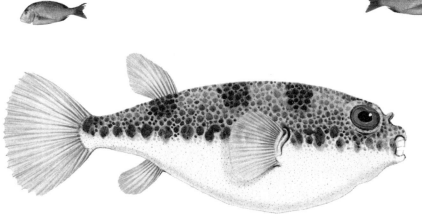

The scourge of the ocean: a dreaded toadfish, the species that evened up with the author in the most embarrassing way.

sun was coming up he boated a nice snapper of around 7 kilograms. By mid-morning he'd caught an assortment of reef fish which included nannygai, sergeant baker and morwong. I hadn't had a bite.

By lunchtime I was starting to wonder if I had leprosy. Then I had a solid bite and hooked up. It was a heavy fish; it seemed that it was its bulk rather than its fighting ability that kept me busy on the 6 kilogram line for about 10 minutes.

At last it was alongside the boat. Thommo got between me and the fish, which I was yet to see, and netted it. 'Struth, mate,' he yelled. 'What a whopper. It's the biggest toadfish I've ever seen in my life. You'll win a prize with this one for sure.'

Toadfish? What the bloody hell was a toadfish? I was soon to find out. Thommo lifted the net and emptied its contents into the bottom of the boat. Oh no!!!! I couldn't believe my eyes. It was the biggest blowie I had ever seen in my life. So that's what they called blowies in the eastern states – toadfish. It must have been 60 centimetres long and weighed about 4 kilograms. And there it was, smiling up at me from the deck with its buck teeth, grunting and puffing and farting as if to say, 'Hello, Paul, haven't you been expecting me?'

No, I hadn't. Yuk! Memories of all the unspeakable things I had done to his ancestors came flooding back, and my father's words were ringing in my ears: 'It's called "karma", son.'

'Good on you, mate,' Thommo said. 'We'll weigh that in and you can bet that no one else will catch a toady bigger than that. That's if anyone catches one at all. They're pretty rare around here.'

So rare that I'd never heard anyone mention them before. 'But I can't weigh a blowie,' I protested.

'Rubbish,' he said. 'The contest says the biggest of *any* species and that's a *species*. You'll get a good cash prize.'

Under protest he put the vile, grunting, blurting beast into the capture bag with his assortment of reef fish and we headed in for the weigh-in at Watsons Bay, where a huge crowd, including press photographers and TV cameramen, had gathered. As Thommo and I had started favourites, we got a big cheer as we carried the huge bag full of fish to the scales. The onlookers oohed and aahed and cheered and applauded as Thommo produced fish after fish, all of which took out the prizes in their field.

'Come on mate, it's your turn now,' Thommo called to me. There was only one giant bulge left in the bag, and the crowd hummed in anticipation. But their sighs of enthusiasm turned to shrieks of laughter as I up-ended the bag and the giant blowie rolled along the ground, collecting grass cuttings all along its body. When it finally came to a stop it looked for all the world like a slimy, green, grinning lamington.

The weighmaster, Ken Hanly, held the stinking thing up by its tail. The crowd chanted in unison, 'Toady, toady, toady', and all pointed at me. 'Come on, Paul, you should know better than to try to weigh this rotten thing,' he said above the laughter. 'You should know as well as I do that they've been outlawed in fishing comps in every state for donkey's years.'

I looked at Thommo, who had collapsed laughing. I'd been set up beautifully, and I had to cop it sweet or be a bad sport. The blowies had had their revenge. It took me a long time to live it down, and to this day I cringe whenever anyone yells out 'toady'.

My old dad was right. So let this be a lesson to all of you out there who are cruel to dumb animals: they will always come back to get you in some form or another.

The Last of the Shark Hunters

*I grew up and fished with most of the old-timers,
and listened in awe to their stories of great sea
creatures and how they went about catching and killing
them. My friend Stewart Donaldson was one of those
wonderful characters who spent the last years of his life
preaching conservation of the oceans rather than killing.*

He was getting on a bit, the old shark hunter. But even at 83, Stewart Donaldson's memory was as sharp as ever, and he recalled epic battles with mammoth sea monsters as if they were yesterday.

Stewie told tales of huge sharks that defied the imagination, sharks that were totally fearless as they glided up the berley trail and ripped and tore at the slabs of whale blubber hanging from the side of the boat.

Giant-toothed critters with mouths the size of 44 gallon drums that could straighten tempered steel hooks and swallow two men at a time. Cruising cannibals that would eat their brethren at the drop of a hat and have even been known to eat their own entrails.

To the last of the old shark hunters, it was all in a day's sport. Stewie was one of the few survivors of those days in the 1950s when it wasn't frowned upon to use whale blubber as berley and bait to attract and catch the sharks that the public hated with a passion.

Rather than being seen as anti-conservationists and murderers, as they would be today, shark hunters of that era were seen as heroes, and the newsreels and press couldn't get enough of them.

Bob and Dolly Dyer, Alf Dean, Charlie Chambers, Jack Davey, Errol Bullen and Max Lawson were household names. With the exception of Dolly, who lives in retirement on the Gold Coast, they've all gone now, and all Stewie has left are the memories and the scrapbooks.

'In those days there were thousands of humpback whales in a never-ending procession going past Brisbane's Moreton Bay about a quarter of a mile offshore,' Stewie recalled in an interview I conducted with him a few years ago. 'We just assumed they were there for the whale chasers to kill, and then their parts would be used to make oil, soap and even perfumes.

'Whaling was big business, and at Tangalooma whaling station on Moreton Island they would carve up the carcasses, and the blood and offal would be hosed into Moreton Bay.

'It was like whistling in the cows. Sharks would turn up in their thousands – whalers, tigers and giant white pointers – and it was on for young and old as they fought for the scraps.

'You could have walked to the whaling station on their backs; we used to part them with the boat as we called in to get some blubber for berley and bait.

'There was no thought that anyone could be doing the wrong thing by killing the whales, and even less thought for the sharks that were killed in their thousands by amateur anglers in the name of sport. In fact, Bob Dyer had shares in the whaling industry.'

Born in Forestville, in New South Wales, Stewart spent most of his early years fishing around Sydney for blackfish. He always had a fascination for sharks and read everything he could find about them. It was this knowledge that got him onto the shark boats in the first place.

'I was at Watsons Bay one Sunday watching Bob Dyer weigh a few sharks he'd caught off Sydney,' he recalled. 'The joint was lousy with them in those days and I said to Dyer's boatman, Basil Davidson, "That's a nice couple of bronze whalers and a tiger."

'Basil was surprised at my textbook knowledge of sharks and told me

that the famous fisherman of the day, Max Lawson, was looking for a crewman. I rang Max, got the job, and fished out of Sydney with him on Thursdays, Saturdays and Sundays.

'We caught every type of shark imaginable – tigers, makos, whalers, white pointers, hammerheads – and other gamefish, such as marlin and tuna,' Stewart said.

'But all the publicity was coming out of Moreton Bay, where Dyer was bringing in up to 10 sharks a day and catching white pointers weighing over 900 kilograms. We decided to go up and take a look.

'Four of us took all our fishing gear, chartered a 20 metre trawler out of Moreton Bay and moored for a week at a time at Yellow Patch, on the tip of Moreton Island, in 15 metres of water. The fishing was unbelievable – thousands of sharks and any amount of huge snapper and kingfish hovering underneath them.

'We hung huge pieces of blubber on ropes on the sides of the boat. As the rocking dipped them in and out of the water, huge tigers and whites would compete to bite them. In order to beat the others to the blubber, the white pointers would come head and shoulders out of the water to get at it first. That was a very scary sight.

The old shark hunter with a huge hook almost straightened out by a giant white pointer.

'The whites were the cheekiest of the lot. I remember one day Dick Rowe was hand-lining for snapper when a huge white pointer launched itself in through the tuck at the back of the boat and almost grabbed him by the legs. Dick went the colour of the yellow spray jacket he was wearing, and I don't blame him.'

While thousands of sharks in the area offered sport all day long, Stewie recalled it being the white pointers that were hunted the most.

'The world-famous angler Zane Grey had christened them "the great white death". Public interest was aroused, and the more of them we killed and strung up on the gantry, the more people turned out to herald us as heroes.

'We could bring in tigers and whalers up to 500 kilograms, but they wanted to see the huge whites. And they were nasty bastards of things. One day I caught a 400 kilogram whaler, and had it hanging off the side of the boat. A monster white came along and ate it in three bites – and the whaler was still alive. That white would have been 5 metres long and weighed more than 1000 kilograms.

'At night we would try to sleep as the huge whites bashed against the boat, gorging themselves on the carcasses of tigers and whalers we had hanging off the side.

'I have no regret about what we did in those times,' he said. 'There were plenty of sharks and whales around and they were there for the killing. That was how we were brought up.

'But these days I'm against the killing, because if we continue the way we are, there will be no great sea creatures left. The difference between what's out there now and what we used to see only 40 years ago is astonishing. And if it's allowed to go on, in another 40 years there will be nothing.

'Yes, the killing had to stop,' he said. And in time it did.

Stewie Donaldson passed away in September 1997. As requested by Stewie, I delivered his eulogy and read excerpts from the next story in this book, 'The Day of the Great White Death', which involved him. His ashes were thrown into the sea to be with the great sea creatures forever.

The last of the old shark hunters is at rest.

The Day of the Great White Death

These days white pointers are a protected species. But in bygone days they were regarded as the enemy, and brave men and women put to sea to capture them and hang them up for all to see. This is one of their stories.

'Stewart, come quickly!' Grace Donaldson called to her husband. 'I think we're drifting onto a reef.' He was at her side in an instant. The dark shape beneath the boat brought back many memories. None of them good.

'That's no reef, woman. That's a great white shark!' he exclaimed. Grace paled at the thought.

Next thing, the 'reef' was alongside the boat. With one bite it bit in half a 400 pound whaler that was hanging from the side.

Many times Stewart had told stories of these mammoth fish that know no fear and are as cold-bloodedly casual as the deadliest of killers.

Now he looked death in the eye as the huge fish rolled and lunged at the remains of the stricken whaler. It lifted itself head and shoulders out of the water, a trick the whites use to snatch sleeping seals off the rocks in the southern waters. Another mouthful of whaler and the huge fish slid back below the surface.

Grace helped the men clear the deck, then took up residence in the cabin as the crew went to work. All lines were brought in and Charlie

Chambers hurriedly baited a giant hook with the remains of the whaler's tail. He attached the wire trace to the 130 pound outfit and floated it out in the direction of the huge fish, now mooching around in the berley.

Bob Head took the wheel while Basil Davidson prepared to throw the dan buoy if there were a hook-up. At first it seemed that the shark was not interested in the bait. He cruised past, heading back towards the boat, his huge dorsal cutting the chop.

Then with one swish of his awesome tail he did a full 180 degree turn. In a second he was on the bait, wolfing it down. Charlie let him get it right down before he set the hook. Strike!! The big diesels roared to life and the dan buoy was thrown. The fight was on ...

The events leading up to this started on Anzac Day 1956. The Max Lawson-owned *Murrawolga* was moored up on Long Reef Wide, northeast of Sydney Heads. Max was marching in the Anzac Day parade so the crew headed out without him.

Basil Davidson had taken the first strike – a whaler of 450 pounds. Basil drew the short straw again, and soon another larger whaler was tied alongside. Bob Head was next in the chair. Yet another big whaler. Non-stop action now, and Stewart Donaldson soon had an out-of-season marlin of 190 pounds secured to the bollard.

Then it went quiet. The baits remained untouched for an hour. The men drank and played cards in the cabin while Grace Donaldson hand-lined for snapper ... until Mr Big arrived ...

Charlie Chambers kisses the white pointer he caught off Long Reef.

46

Charlie leaned back into the huge split-can rod. The sheer bulk of the predator had him awestruck. The fish was very aware that something was wrong; it was rolling up in the trace and thrashing around near the surface. Then it made a series of long runs that had smoke pouring from the Hardy reel. The crew cooled the angler and the reel with buckets of water.

For an hour the fish doggedly headed east, with the *Murrawolga* in hot pursuit, gaining line at every opportunity. Just when they thought the fight was over the fish would head off again, peeling line from the reel whenever it desired. The cuttyhunk cord held.

Charlie knew his trade well. Not once was the pressure taken off the fish. Each time it looked like taking more line than necessary the angler leaned back hard on the thick rod to let his adversary know who was dictating the terms. Several times they feared the shark had been lost as it entangled itself in the trace and double line. But each time the line miraculously came out unscathed.

One hour and 40 minutes of backbreaking struggle had the fish back at the side of the boat.

'Basil's on the wire – you're first gaff, Stewie,' Charlie commanded. Basil's gloved hands wrapped the wire as Bob reversed the boat towards the fish.

Stewart reached out across the shark's width to secure the vital first gaff, but the girth of the fish was immense – the gaff couldn't make the distance, and the sharp point kept skidding off the shark's back.

'He's too big, Charlie,' Stewart called. 'We'll have to risk a mouth gaff.' Charlie leapt from the chair and disconnected the flying head of the gaff from the handle. Poised near the snapping jaws, he waited for the right moment to place it in the shark's mouth. Having done so, Stewart pulled the rope taut and the giant gaff head penetrated the upper jaw.

'At least we've got one end of him secure,' Stewart commented. 'The other half isn't going to be so easy.'

The boat was taking a pounding. The shark's tail was thrashing and hammering at the gunwale. The crew were drenched. Charlie hung firm on the mouth gaff rope.

'Get another on in the mid-section if you can,' he called to Stewart. The shot was good. The gaff went cleanly into the lower underbelly. Still the giant fish wreaked havoc. If something wasn't done soon, either the ropes would snap or the bollards would break.

At this stage the fish's head was securely tied halfway up the boat, but its enormous length had the tail trailing 2 metres beyond the stern. Only a tail rope would secure their prize. 'You're going to have to go over the side, Stewie,' Charlie grimaced. 'It's the only way we're going to get a rope around his tail.'

Under normal circumstances you would prefer to be stuck in an alley with Jack the Ripper, but now was not the time for indecision. Stewart was held by the feet and lowered out to the shark's tail. He floated the huge lasso around it and pulled tight. The fish was theirs. Another two tail ropes and the battle was over.

They radioed to base that they were bringing in a huge shark. Word spread quickly. People turned out in their thousands to watch the weigh-in. In the terms of that era it tipped the scales at 2100 pounds. That's just under 1000 kilograms!! The great white was 4.90 metres long and 4.88 metres around the girth.

To this day it is the largest fish ever taken in Sydney waters. Charlie Chambers died in 1976. He ashes were scattered at Long Reef Wide.

The Loaded Croc

*Although this story may be a few years old now,
it is Sydney Eastern Suburbs folklore, and while
the variations of it are many, this is the
fair dinkum version. Though conspicuous by
their absence in recent years, the main characters are
real and the story never came to light until long after
the incident – one day the two of them had a
monumental altercation at the Royal Oak Hotel and
one blurted out just how stupid his mate was, giving
this story as an example.*

We christened him 'Haemorrhoids' because he hung out in dark places. We broke it down to 'Piles' for short. One of those dark places he hung out in was the old front bar of the Royal Oak Hotel in Double Bay, in Sydney's Eastern Suburbs, where he was a member of the legendary Royal Oak Fishing Club.

He was a bald, short, unshaven revoltingly fat heap with a Charles Bronson drooping moustache. He wore Stubbies and a football jumper every day, guzzled vast quantities of beer and wore out two pairs of thongs a month.

The locals reckoned that one day when he was lying on Bondi Beach the Greenpeace truck came to a grinding halt and six guys rushed out and tried to force him back into the water.

The only person who could cop him was a bloke we'd nicknamed 'Morphine', on account of the fact that he was a slow-working dope. Morph was as long and lean as Piles was short and rotund, wore a Sydney Swans beanie, checked long-sleeved flannelette shirts, flared trousers and ugh boots all year round.

Standing at the bar they looked like Abbott and Costello, outfitted by the local St Vincent de Paul shop's reject bin.

Piles and Morph were inseparable, and quaffed down schooners night after night over the pool table at the Oak. And when they weren't playing pool or figuring out how to get away with more sickies from their jobs as road workers on the local council, they filled out their weekly Lotto coupon, methodically double and triple checking to make sure that they got their lucky numbers – which, incidentally, were the same every week – exactly right.

They figured they would have the winning combination by using the numbers that meant the most to them. Their birth dates: 16 and 24; their ages: 37 and 39; their IQs (from the council's test): 28 and 28; their past lovers: 0 and 0; and their friends: 1 and 1, being each other.

So that was the combination: 16, 24, 37, 39, 28 and 0, with 1 as the supplementary. Week in and week out they took the same numbers, and every Monday night at 8.30 the Oak would come to a standstill as the beautiful Alex Wileman called the numbers with the three lotteries officials looking on.

But they never won a crumpet. In fact the best they ever got was two numbers. But their faith in their system was unfailing.

This particular Monday, Morph had taken a sickie and got on the turps; he was horribly flyblown by the time he filled in the Lotto numbers. And then he had a dozen or so more schooners at the Oak while waiting for his mate to come in after work.

When Morph produced their ticket at Lotto time, Piles nearly had a stroke.

'You fuckin' idiot,' he exploded. You've written out the wrong numbers. I couldn't trust you to take a piss by yourself. You can bet your fuckin' life they'll go off tonight and we won't be on 'em.'

With that he grabbed a snooker cue in one hand and Morph by the throat with the other … he was just about to fracture his dopey mate's skull with it when Alex Wileman called out the first number – 17.

'Hey, that's one of your bodgie numbers,' Piles noted, lowering the cue and taking interest. 'Number 4,' the sensational Alex Wileman gushed as Piles noted that that number was also on the ticket.

And so was the next one, and the one after that and the one after that. They had the first five numbers. The Oak was hushed in anticipation. Alex called the sixth number and it matched the ticket – the pub went berserk.

The Dickbrain Brothers had won Lotto by default, but Morph wasn't letting on that it was a fluke.

'It's me new scientific system of gettin' the numbers,' he told anyone stupid enough to listen. 'I'd had 17 schooners when I bought the ticket; me nephew's four next birthday …' and so on. Of course no one with an eighth of a brain took any notice.

There turned out to be three other winners, but even when the four split the $1.5 million first prize, Piles and Morph still had easily enough to buy the best Toyota 4WD, camping gear and trailerable boat that money could buy. They decided to go on an extended fishing vacation to northern Australia, much to our eternal gratitude.

'That'll teach you pricks to take the piss out of us,' Piles announced down at the Oak on the eve of their departure as he begrudgingly threw a lousy $20 on the bar. 'Me and me genius mate 'ere, Morph, is gonna shoot through to the Northern Territory and get stuck into the barramundis and none of you billygoats is welcome.

And thank Christ for that. Peace from the boneheads at last. Even if it was only temporary.

It took Piles and Morphine six days to reach Darwin, where they loaded up with cases of beer and supplies and headed for the Mary River. They found a great big barra-filled lagoon and set up camp.

What a treat. No bastard for miles, stacks of ice in the freezer for the beer, no sheilas to drive 'em mad and a hole full of fish. Heaven on earth. Well, not quite.

There was just one minor problem – the old croc who'd made the huge billabong his home for the past 30 years. The cranky old bastard was far from impressed with his new neighbours and expressed his disapproval by nicking every decent-sized fish they hooked.

'There's that fuckin' mobile suitcase at it again,' Morphine would blubber to his mate as the croc sat waiting for a jumping barra to land in its giant, foul-smelling gob-hole.

'I wish he'd fuck off and leave us alone,' moaned Piles as he lost yet another barra, a $15 lure and lots of line to the croc.

But they were reluctant to move on, because the fishing – minus the croc – was about as good as it gets. Besides, there would most likely be a resident croc wherever they wound up. Sooner or later something had to give. It did.

'Have you noticed how he shoots through every night around six?' noted Piles, his skills of observation working overtime. 'I reckon he goes back to the missus in the lair, chunders up some of the fish he's pinched from us and feeds it to 'er, gives 'er a good root and then packs it in for the night.'

'The dirty bastard – I'd like to blow his scaly old cock off while he's on the job!'

They laughed hilariously at the thought of two crocodiles hard at it, and wondered if they tongue-kissed each other while they were doing it, what with their abundance of teeth and bad breath.

Neither of them was renowned for his powers of deduction, so while the thought of a prehistoric animal living to a timetable would be absurd to most of us, it certainly wasn't to Piles and his dopey mate. Instead, it gave one of them an idea.

'Speakin' of blowin' the bastard's dick off, you've given me a real good idea,' Piles chuckled to his mate. 'Let's go into town tomorrow and I'll get somethin' that might just sort our problem right out. He'll be a cockless croc come dusk.'

In town the following morning they loaded up with supplies, then ducked into the hardware store. They bought a case of dynamite and all the other ingredients they needed to blow up fish-stealing, prehistoric reptiles.

'Do you really think it'll work?' Morph asked his mate, plainly in awe of the brilliant scheme.

'Course it will,' said Piles. 'We wait until the bastard comes up for his last fish of the arvo and we'll chuck him a couple of nicely iced-off barra out of the big Esky under the 4WD.

'Only this time they'll have enough dynamite attached to blow up fuckin' Ayers Rock.

'Once the greedy prick of a thing has swallowed the lot, we'll let him swim off with the fuse wire trailing out of his gob, and when he stops we'll wait till we reckon he's on the job and then we'll light it, and give his missus the biggest bang she's ever had.'

They laughed uproariously at their scheme and went about fishing from the bank, well down the river from their campsite, and preparing themselves for the afternoon's events. And as if on cue, the croc did his bit by turning up and pinching their fish all day long.

'Go on make the most of it, ya fuckin' turd of a thing,' Morph abused the old croc from the bank. 'Ya might as well, seein' as today's ya last day on this planet. In a coupla hours your head's gonna be in Darwin and ya cock's gonna be in Alice Springs.'

Mid-afternoon they returned to the camp, grabbed a couple of nice cold barramundi from the Esky under the Land Cruiser and taped four sticks of dynamite to them with electrician's tape.

Just on six they hooked a beaut fish that brought the crocodile within feeding range. As he gulped the leaping barra down, Piles threw the dynamited fish at him – he gulped those down too.

'The silly prick's fallen for it,' laughed Morphine. 'You're a bloody genius, Piles. Now let's wait for a while and we'll teach the bastard to pinch our fish.'

So they sat on the bank and watched as the waterproofed fuse wire steadily reeled off the giant coil and into the water as the croc headed off upstream.

They'd bought plenty of beer and it was only a five-minute trip by boat back to camp. They yarned the time away as the croc kept on the move.

'It'll be interestin' just to see where the explosion goes off,' said Piles. 'Christ, he must have 1000 metres of fuse wire out by now. One thing's for certain – the big bang won't be close to us.'

Then the croc stopped. They waited for a couple of minutes, then lit the fuse and watched the smoke snake down the bank and into the water.

'I hope he's on the vinegar stroke when it goes off,' roared Piles. 'That'll make the earth move for Mrs Croc in a manner she wasn't counting on!'

Then it happened. The bank shook as a huge explosion rocked the earth all around and a mushroom-shaped ball of smoke belched high into the sky from downriver – in the direction of the camp.

They took off in the boat at breakneck speed amid falling debris, only some of it flesh and blood.

'Jesus, that was a big bit,' Piles gulped at a huge splash near them. 'And it didn't look like a blown-up croc to me. It looked more like a gearbox. A Toyota gearbox.'

Morphine ducked just in time to avoid decapitation by a flying steering wheel. As they raced towards camp they realised that their worst nightmare had come to pass.

'You fuckin' idiot!' screamed Morph at Piles.

'You gave that croc a taste for cold barramundi and the bastard's crawled up to the Esky for more! You've blown our bloody truck into the Kimberley! How are we gonna get home?'

As it turned out, this was the least of their worries. That evening they were arrested for violations of the Protection of Crocodiles Act and their return to Double Bay was interrupted by a stay in the Darwin nick.

Both Morphine and Haemorrhoids are barred from the Northern Territory for life.

Fish with Teeth

It is a little-known fact that not all fish have teeth. In fact I'd go as far as to say that there would be as many gormless fish as there are ones with choppers. Mind you, in that mysterious world beneath the waves where it's a case of the one with the longest and sharpest teeth wins, if I were a fish I'd much rather have a mouthful of crockery than not.

For openers, kingfish, marlin and most of the tunas don't have teeth, though it is interesting to note that a marlin's beak is made up of millions of minuscule teeth that can only be seen under a microscope.

Sailfish, trevally, trout and garfish don't have teeth, but coral trout, bream, snapper and barracouta do. Mullet don't need them because they were put on this planet to be eaten by toothy critters rather than to do the eating.

Tailor are most certainly fanged. Their nickname – 'choppers' – comes from their ability to use their razor-sharp teeth to chop the tails off their prey, rendering them helpless and allowing the tailor to pounce on and eat them.

But then again, tailor themselves are much sought after by predators such as jewfish, kingfish, tuna and salmon, and when there's a school of tailor getting into the baitfish you can bet your life that there's a bunch of bigger predators waiting in the wings to get stuck into them.

Whiting have small teeth for chomping open pipis and other crustaceans they find while fossicking along the bottom, and flathead have small yet effectively sharp fangs for munching on their favourite tucker – small whiting.

Bream use their teeth and powerful jaws to crack open oysters, mussels and crustaceans to get a feed. Snapper use that big bump on their noggins to bash oysters and other morsels from reefs; then they munch on them with their molars to get at the succulent meat inside.

Only a couple of the common tunas have teeth: the bonito and a horrifying aquatic gangster called the dogtooth tuna. The doggy is well named, because its craw is a dentist's nightmare, full of needle-sharp daggers. Combine this with the dogtooth's determination to escape when hooked and its ravenous appetite, and you have one of the most formidable critters ever to swim the oceans.

Baitfish such as pilchards, yellowtail, slimy mackerel and whitebait don't have teeth because, like the mullet, they were put here by Mother Nature to be eaten and not to do the eating.

On the other hand, there are a couple of horrendous biters that are found in and around the Great Barrier Reef and northern Australia: the wahoo and the Spanish mackerel were designed to bite and kill anything that swims, and out of all the ocean's killing machines this pair would

The dogtooth tuna is appropriately named. And once they bite they don't let go.

have to be the Daily Double in speed and killing efficiency. They are long, torpedo-shaped fish that can travel at amazing speeds – especially when zeroing in for the kill. They have triangle-shaped mouths and an assortment of wisdom teeth that could bite through a broomstick.

Up north they call 'em 'the razor gang' because they have the

uncanny ability to cut a whole trolled fish bait in half with their choppers and never get caught on the barb of the hook, which is secreted in the bait's belly, usually about an eighth of an inch in front of the bite.

Off Sydney in the 1970s we caught a 20 kilogram wahoo (which was extremely unusual this far south), brought it on board the boat, whacked it with the donger and put it in the ice box to fillet later and have for dinner – they are as good to eat as they are to catch.

One of our lady crew members lifted the fish out of the box later, and as she did so, she accidentally

The razor-sharp jaws of the Spanish mackerel can bite through a broomstick.

ran its gaping mouth over another lady crew member's leg, cutting the skin to the bone and causing her to be hospitalised and have about 20 stitches. That's how sharp a wahoo's teeth are. They can still get you long after they're dead.

Barramundi don't have teeth, but they don't need them – their huge mouths engulf their prey and then they just swallow them whole.

It seems to me that one of the prerequisites of living in warm waters anywhere in the world is to have long, sharp teeth – and plenty of them. When you look at the type of neighbourhood the fish have to live in, that's quite understandable.

There are so many dangerous characters hanging about that it looks more like the remand yard at Pentridge than a fish paradise. Everything that lives there is out to chew the butt off everything else.

These warm waters are also the haunt of another horrifically toothed denizen of the deep – the barracuda, the only fish that has been known to attack human beings, especially divers.

The barracuda grows to 25 kilograms in tropical waters and has been known to attack humans.

Unlike the wahoo and the mackerel, the barracuda (not to be confused with the southern barra*couta*) has protruding, gripping (rather than biting) front teeth that would make a bull terrier's look like a couple of carpet tacks. And as the nasty old barracuda gets bigger, so do his fangs; by the time he's about a metre long, his two front choppers are as long as concrete nails and could put holes in a baseball bat.

When he gets to this size he becomes known as a *great* barracuda, and it is these whoppers that bite people. They become extremely territorial, the prime predator of a particular reef. Sort of like the local bad guy.

But while lots of divers have been bitten, or at least attacked, experts believe that it is not because the great barracuda likes taking chunks out of human beings. They reckon that in the murky water that is usually what is around during an attack, the barracuda confuses the diver with a fish that it would like to eat. I believe them.

So next time you catch a fish — no matter what species — have a look at the crockery department before you let it go. You'll be surprised what you'll find.

Fish with teeth — Spanish mackerel, sharks, wahoo, tailor, barracuda, barracouta, snapper, bream, dogtooth tuna, bonito, coral trout, whiting, flathead, snapper, red emperor, mangrove jack, pike.

Fish without teeth — Most tuna, sailfish, marlin, trevally, trout, garfish, mullet, barramundi, yellowtail, slimy mackerel, kingfish, salmon, herring.

Fishing Dogs

*Dogs and fishing go together like cats and milk. They
have certainly always been a part of my fishing life, and
I've fished on many a boat where a dog has been a
member of the crew. My search for the ultimate Aussie
fishing dog came up Trumps.*

To my mind, dogs are about the most humorous critters in the
world, and they are as much a part of fishing as your rod and
reel. You know the old saying: 'A dog is a man's best friend
because he wags his tail and not his tongue.'

They don't do much to help us catch fish, but there's always a dog
somewhere in the typical Aussie fishing scene.

The classic cartoon of the scruffy kid on his way through the bush to
his favourite spot with a fishing pole over his shoulder, a jar of tadpoles
and the inevitable dog at his heels says it all.

The first European dog to lift his leg on Australian soil was a
Newfoundland mutt named Hector, who came here with the First Fleet
and was owned by John Marshall, the master of 450 ton convict
transport *Scarborough*.

I wonder if it was just coincidence that Marshall chose a
Newfoundland – or was it because they were the original fishing dogs?

They went to sea on fishing boats and were trained to swim out to the nets, when they were heavy with salmon, and help the fishermen drag them in.

Did the wise old ship's master anticipate that there would be fish aplenty in the new land and that Hector could help catch them?

If that were the case, Sir Joseph Banks didn't have fishing on his mind when he chose his canine companion for the voyage. At Foreshore Park in Botany Bay, a monument celebrating the fleet's arrival shows Banks examining flora and fauna. At his feet there is a dog that is either a whippet or a greyhound ... it is most certainly not a fishing dog.

But while dogs can be great fishing companions, they can also be bloody pests. I'd like a dollar for every time one has piddled on my fishing bag or run off with the lunch Mum so painstakingly put together.

Years ago there was a dog who used to haunt the wharf at Kurnell on the southern side of Botany Bay. He would pinch the bait and eat it, and he didn't care whether there was a hook in it or not. Anglers got sick of taking hooks out of the poor old fella, but he never learned from the experience. They would take half a dozen hooks out of him one night and he'd be back there the next day for more.

The luckiest ocean-going pooch alive is a four-year-old German shepherd bitch named Lizzy, who was found swimming 6 kilometres off Queensland's Sunshine Coast by two fishermen last November. She was claimed by her relieved owners the following day. They said that Lizzy had fallen, unnoticed, off their yacht and they had given up any hope of seeing her again. The very exhausted Lizzy had been in the shark-infested waters for about six hours when she was rescued.

And then there was Rex the Wonder Dog, who lived at the Gap Tavern on top of the cliffs at the famous suicide spot at Sydney's Watsons Bay. Many a time Rex saved the lives of potential suicide victims by grabbing their clothing and dragging them back from the cliffs as they stood and contemplated the 120 metre jump.

Buster the fishing dog was the toast of the coast when he performed the most extraordinary rescue while fishing with his master, Gary

Nicholson, off the high rocks at Malabar Point on the northern shores of Botany Bay.

Buster and Gary were fishing away when a nearby rockhopper made such a forceful cast that his rod flew from his hands and landed in the drink. The ever-alert Buster leapt into the water, grabbed the rod between his teeth and braved a dreadful buffeting on the rocks to drop the rod and reel back at the amazed angler's feet.

So with all these dog fishing facts and stories in mind, I set out on a quest to find Sydney's fishiest dog. With my cameras whirring, I searched the beaches and wharves, and though I found plenty of dogs

Trump, the fishing dog, in his favourite angling outfit.

hanging about, none of them had the qualifications to be immortalised in a fishing story book

I let my friends know what I was looking for. A dog who was up to its eyeballs in anything that involved fish.

A big ask? It sure was, but if I was going to go to the trouble to take pictures and write the story, the canine had to have something special.

A fishy dog that went out on trawlers, or helped serve behind the counter at the fishmarkets, perhaps wrestled crocodiles, maybe stood guard at the Oceanarium, or rode a surf ski while his master trolled a hand line off the back, would have been ideal. No such luck.

And then, just when I was about to give up, I found Trump.

Trump is a Dalmatian–blue heeler who lives with the Franks family, Norelle, husband Bill, and daughter Camilla, at Sydney's Watsons Bay. He's a docile old slug, probably due to his being grossly obese – he's well over his fighting weight.

Norelle reckons that if Trump went to Jenny Craig they would only give him a quote. And there's a very good reason for Trump's porky condition, but more about that in a minute.

Trump's a real party dog, and at functions at home, he waddles from guest to guest for a pat; he doesn't mind getting dressed up either, as long as it gets him plenty of attention.

And without a doubt, Trump's fishing outfit is his favourite. He'll sit for hours in his gamefishing cap, sunnies, vest, rod and reel, just to cop all the attention from family and friends. And, naturally, the odd handout.

And why wouldn't Trump love fish and fishing? After all, his staple diet is the best seafood in Australia. Trump lives a stone's throw from Doyle's famous Watsons Bay seafood restaurant, and at any lunchtime he can be found on the promenade botting delicious offerings from the Doyle's patrons.

Trump on the bludge at Doyle's seafood restaurant. It looks as though he's so full he can't fit in another chip.

It's little wonder he's so fat he can hardly walk. Chips, fish, crabs and lobster – Trump gets to sample the lot as generous diners fall for the big brown eyes and the slobbering 'I'll go away if you give me a bit' look. And believe me, it's in the diner's best interest to give Trump something to eat and see him on his way, because the sight of him slobbering giant globules all down his chin is enough to put anyone off their lunch, even a famous Doyle's lunch. It's not a pretty sight.

One customer even put a note around his neck which read: 'Mum, please don't feed me tonight because I might be sick.

I've been eating fish and chips all day and I couldn't possibly be hungry.'

Norelle says that Trump never eats at home anyway. He's too busy socialising and having lunch. When he gets home he's so exhausted he takes his ballooning carcass to bed – he probably dreams about botting seafood at Doyle's the next day.

I wouldn't mind coming back as Trump in my next life. No work, no dieting, no money worries, lots of love and the best seafood in the country every day.

The guy who said 'It's a dog's life' obviously hadn't met Trump.

Heli-fishing to Adventure

I've never been so frightened in my life. There are four things I'm not too happy about – snakes, spiders, guns and killing animals – and here I was in the middle of the whole lot of 'em. I could see my life flashing before me.

'There they are,' big Billy McLeod had said. He pointed as I strained my eyes from the back seat of the four-seater Robinson 44 chopper to get my first glimpse of a mobile line of black dots that was a feral pig family on the march.

It was a procession of 15 wild porkers, trunking and tailing across an open sandy causeway that led from one heavily vegetated island to another in the vast interconnecting network of swamplands that made up this pork chop paradise. We were on the outskirts of a private cattle station inland from the sea on the eastern side of Cape York Peninsula, in far northern Queensland.

As the chopper banked in for a closer look, the black dots picked up speed. At the head were nana and pop, then the sons and daughters, followed closely by the grandkids, with the great-grandkids making up the rear. Four generations of the scourge of northern Australia on the run – big Billy was going to do his bit for conservation by blasting the whole lot of them into the next postcode.

Adventuring with a helicopter takes the angler to fish-filled hotspots that are inaccessible by land.

'I'll drop you guys off on that island up ahead, the one they're heading for,' said our pilot, Captain Dennis 'Brazakka' Wallace, marlin fisherman, hunter and adventurer.

'Paul, throw your cameras around your neck and jump out with Billy when I tell you. After I've dropped you guys off, I'm going to circle back, herd them towards you and round up the stragglers and the ones that try to get away.

'Make sure you're ready with the cameras, 'cos Billy'll start pickin' 'em off as soon as they hit the island and I'm safely way-to-buggery out of there.'

I didn't have a chance to protest, or even contemplate what was in the undergrowth on that island. If I was going to die, it seemed I wasn't even going to know what sort of snake or spider it was that bit me!

And then we were there, dumped straight into knee-high undergrowth. If Elle McPherson had been 100 metres away, in the nude, beckoning to me, and the only thing between us was knee-high undergrowth, I'd never get to see that magnificent body up close. I hate undergrowth and all the creepy crawlies that live in it.

As soon as the chopper hit the ground, big Billy was off and running through the undergrowth, a box of shells the size of roll-on deodorants in one hand, a silver 270 Ruger bolt-action rifle in the other, and me desperately trying to fill his every footprint and at the same time stop my cameras from swinging full circle around my neck.

My heart was jumping out of my chest.

Billy propped himself up behind a bush and loaded the bazooka. 'Just stick with me,' he mumbled, obviously under the delusion that I might wander off and take in the sights. No chance. I was sticking to him like shit to a blanket.

'And keep quiet,' he growled. 'They're heading straight towards us and I'm gonna get the big bastards first. Don't let 'em know we're here.'

Having no idea what to expect, except that any second now I was going to be witness to wholesale slaughter, I readied my camera with the wide angle lens and tried to control the gasping that was forcing my heart out of my mouth.

Brazakka and Billy with a haul of barramundi taken from a river mouth on the turn of the tide.

Then they were upon us, running straight at Billy, oinking and puffing and oblivious to the fact that in a minute or two they would all be spare ribs for their relatives to gorge themselves on.

KABOOOM! As the first of the herd hit dry ground about 20 metres in front of him, Billy let fly like the cannon off the *Missouri*, and a giant boar with gravy-stained 15 centimetre tusks, still moving with the momentum of running for its life, lurched towards me and fell almost at my feet, squealing and farting as blood sprayed high into the air from the gaping wound in its neck. It shook its trotters for a second or two, looked up at me, and died.

I wanted to throw up but I didn't have the time. KABOOM! Nana hit the deck minus half her head. KABOOM, KABOOM, mum and dad were dispatched, and it was time to reload and finish off the kids. Fifteen shots – 15 dead pigs.

It was like a scene out of *Apocalypse Now*, with me as Dennis Hopper clicking away amidst the gunsmoke, the stench of Av-gas, the whirling of the descending chopper, and surrounded by death, too shell-shocked to talk, instead letting the camera tell the tale.

I was a gibbering mess when I crawled back into the chopper, leaving the carnage in my wake. 'Looks like you got the lot, Billy,' Brazakka said casually. 'We'll come back here tomorrow. Those carcasses are terrific bait, Paul. We'll get a bunch of their best friends eating 'em tomorrow.

'They're bloody filthy things, those pigs. They're riddled with disease, and when they're not taking calves they're rooting up the environment. Can't shoot enough of the bastards for my money. All right, boys. How about we go and catch a fish?'

That suited me down to the ground.

I was halfway through the first day of a three-day heli-fishing and hunting safari, courtesy of Brazakka. 'Better get your arse up here and take some pictures and write a few stories about my new venture,' he had told me over the phone from his deer ranch on the Atherton Tablelands, just out of Cairns.

Better known as one of the top black marlin skippers in the world, with a track record of over 100 giant marlin in excess of the benchmark

1000 pounds either captured or tagged and released for his stable of famous anglers (which included US president at the time, Jimmy Carter, Lee Marvin and novelist Wilbur Smith), anything Brazakka does is news, and I've been taking pictures and writing stories about him and his adventures for donkey's years.

I knew that the heli-fishing and hunting safaris would be like anything else Brazakka put his hand to – action-packed adventure and bundles of fun.

'I'm running three-day safaris out of Cairns to Cape York for two clients at a time to fish and hunt,' he told me. 'It's about as much action as anyone can cope with in three days, and we cover more territory than you'd ever see out of a 4WD in two weeks. You'll get some great shots.'

He wasn't wrong. We had left Cairns that morning and flown along the coast to Cooktown, our first stop for fuel. Big Billy McLeod, ace angler, crack shot and an authority on Cape York and its fishing holes, was along for the ride, pointing out places he had either fished or hunted over the years.

We'd stopped briefly on the golden sands of Princess Charlotte Bay for a feed of prawns Billy had brought with him, and then we flew on up the coast, noting the best spots to fish – where the tidal rivers and creeks feed into the ocean and the barramundi, king salmon, mangrove jacks and tarpon lay in wait as the baitfish are forced out with the tide.

'The run-out isn't until mid-afternoon,' Billy had calculated. 'Let's go and kill us a few pigs while we wait.'

And kill pigs Billy did until it was time to head back to the coast and catch the fish napping while they were waiting for afternoon tea on the turn of the tide.

'That spot should do us,' said Brazakka, pointing to a big lagoon with fast-running water and a 5 metre croc basking on the sand, guarding its manor against unwelcome intruders. As we approached to land it opened its gob, which could have passed for the entrance to Luna Park, hissed at us and slid into the drink, obviously not keen to challenge the chopper.

'It's great that we've seen that horrible bastard,' said Billy as Brazakka landed right next to the huge webbed footprints in the sand. 'He knows

we're here and we know *he's* here,' he laughed. 'He's just as frightened of us as we are of him, so now it's a standoff.

'We're safe to fish here until he figures out some sort of a game plan to get us,' Billy continued as he reached down to wash his hands where the footprints disappeared into the lagoon. The hairs on the back of my neck stood on end. I had visions of the croc materialising out of the water in front of him, Crocodile Dundee/Linda Kozlowski style, and Brazakka running in and stabbing it in the head with a Bowie knife. This pair would get off on something like that.

'He's probably over there in the mangroves, sulking,' Billy pointed, now standing ankle deep in the same spot, 'and you can bet your life that if we came back here every day at the same time, after three or four days that old croc would have it all figured out. He'd be waiting just under the surface at the water's edge or somewhere behind one of us, ready to charge and take us with him into the lagoon. They're cunning bastards, but it takes 'em a while to put it together. We'll be long gone by then.'

Billy cast his lure towards a submerged tree that acted as perfect cover for the ambushing barras, cranked his baitcaster into gear, wound the handle a couple of turns and hooked up to a 4 kilo-gram barra. As simple as that.

'Yeah Brazak, they're on,' he mumbled nonchalantly to his mate, who by now had a lure in the water and was also hooked up. 'They should be bitin' their heads off for about another half hour or so, then they'll go off the bite when the tide turns.'

And guess what? They did. I suppose we caught about twenty in that session. It was almost a fish

Threadfin salmon are another prize from northern Australian waters.

Billy lines up the feral pigs while Brazakka keeps an eye on them from the chopper.

a throw. They were so thick that I put down the camera and caught a few myself.

And then, as Billy predicted, there were none. Time to move on.

That night we stayed at an out-station on a remote cattle ranch, drank beer with the locals, dined on steak, eggs and chips, and slept like dead people.

After a huge breakfast the following morning, washed down with real tea made in a big pot with tea leaves floating around in it, it was time for some jungle creek fishing for barramundi, jungle perch, sooty grunter and mangrove jacks.

Jungle fishing is adventure fishing at its best and most difficult: hiking through thick undergrowth, looking for lagoons in a river that has been land-locked since the last wet season, with fish trapped until the next Wet arrives. Then the rains fill the river to overflowing and it and its inhabitants run downstream into the sea.

The hardest part is finding enough room to cast your lure at a snag, which is where the barra and jacks like to hide and ambush their own

meals. Getting to these aquariums in a 4WD is all but impossible, but in a helicopter it's simple to access lagoons that no man has ever fished before. We caught a stack of jacks and barra that day in about twenty different spots.

That night we stayed at a country pub, ate some of the fish we had caught that day for dinner, washed them down with a couple of cold bottles of sauvignon blanc and slept in air-conditioned comfort in bunkhouse-style accommodation. Country living at its best.

On Day 3 we fished and hunted our way home, this time shooting pigs on the grassy savannas – this made taking pictures a lot easier, even if I did have one eye through the lens and the other on the lookout for taipans.

We explored running rivers and creeks, drank crystal-clear water from rocky mountain streams and cast lures into the lagoons.

Lunch on the last day was yet another of the many highlights of the trip. We called into a remote fishing camp on the Annie River and ate delicious warm mud crabs – straight out of the pot – with fresh bread and butter, washed down with icy cold beers. Yummo.

The muddies had been caught and cooked especially for us that morning. It's all part of the deal. The old Brazakka doesn't miss a trick when it comes to giving his clients the trip of a lifetime.

If there is a problem with the trip, it's that so much happens in the three days that it's hard to remember what happened a few hours earlier. Usually hunting and fishing just don't go hand in hand, even though most hunters are anglers and vice versa. Combine the two with the convenience of a chopper and it's a once in a lifetime blow-out. Even for an old city slicker like me.

The Fish Hit Parade

What could be more logical than using wonderful sea noises to attract fish? But what do you do when they get sick of the same old sounds? You should give them a choice, that's what. And if this piscatorial lunacy doesn't get you making up a few tunes yourself, then your funny bone should go into the berley pot.

Many years ago we invented the Fish Hit Parade. That's right. A piscatorial parade of pops for pilchards, piranhas, prawns, pike and perch. Crazy? Maybe. But it's also lots of fun and helps while away the hours when the fish aren't biting. And let's face it … that's usually most of the time.

It all started when I read a few years back that someone had invented this gadget that attracted tuna to the professional boats. It worked like this. They figured that if they could replicate some sounds that attracted the tuna, the tuna would follow those soundwaves to the source, in this case a giant tuna trawler, and they could be caught. Instead of going to the tuna, wherever they were, these guys would bring the tuna to them.

And they did this by lowering into the water a transmitter that sent out sounds that were music to the tuna's ears – the sounds of millions

of anchovies or pilchards boiling in the water, for example. Or the noises of thousands of sea birds screeching and flapping their wings as they plummeted into the water to feed on the baitfish. Or the sounds of distressed fish sending out vibrations through the currents. Ingenious.

♪♪♫♪ Salmon Chanted Evening ♪♪♫♪

What's even more incredible is that it worked! The tuna would flock to the transmitter like Brown's cows. Then the skipper would turn the sound up. This would whip them into a frenzy, and the crew would just pole them into the boat. As simple as that.

It worked for a couple of years, and then the tuna didn't come any more. No one could figure it out. Had they caught them all? Had the tuna gone to warmer or colder currents?

One balmy Sunday afternoon many years later, during the NSW Inter-Club Gamefishing Tournament, we were sucking on some cold beers and trolling the current lines of Port Stephens for marlin on Keith Whitehead's *Splashdown* when someone commented on the shortage of fish and wondered where they had gone.

It reminded me of the disappearing tuna all those years ago, so I told the fellas the story.

'Maybe they got sick of hearing the same music over and over again,' commented the skipper, Darcy Franklin. 'They probably woke up to the fact that they were being conned and shot through. They should have played 'em something different.'

'Like what?' said deckie John Whitehead, '*Salmon Chanted Evening* perhaps? Or maybe *Mullet of Kintyre?*'

♪♪♫♪ *I Did it Mulloway* ♪♫♫♪

'How about *I Did it Mulloway?*' said Darcy. The Fish Hit Parade was born.

We spent the rest of the day racking our brains for more and came up with the obvious ones like: *I'm Breaming of a Whiting Christmas, When You Said You Loved Me I Thought I Was Herring Things, Twist and Trout, Whale Meat Again* and *I Lobster and Never Flounder Again.*

Back at the pub we had the joint in hysterics, and the drunker we got, the cornier and funnier the Fish Hit Parade became. *Tunny Boy* brought the house down and *Prawn Free* and *Slimy to the Moon* had 'em rolling in the aisles.

It was one of the funniest nights that the Country Club Hotel at Shoal Bay has ever seen.

And then the tournament was over and it was time to go home. The Fish Hit Parade was put on hold until the following year, but by then it seemed to have lost its momentum – it just didn't seem as funny as when we invented it.

I published a short story about the Fish Hit Parade and listed the old favourites, most of which I have already mentioned. Expecting little or no response, I was bewildered when letters started pouring in from all over the country with lists of songs to be included in a revised and updated version of the fish's Top Ten.

Andrew Campbell-Burns, of Melbourne, sent in no less than 52 titles, and a Colonel Alan Durant and his mate, Patrolman Terry King, produced 32 fishy favourites.

With many thanks to them, lots of other readers and Brad, John and Darcy, I have now compiled the world exclusive Fish Hit Parade of the

Twenty-one All-Time Classics (and added on some composers and groups who are worth a mention):

A White Cork Float And A Pink Crustacean
Oyster Her Standing There
On the Toad to Manta Ray
Flake, Rattle and Troll
I Love Her But I Just Can't Kipper Any More
You Make My Life Halibut I'm Staying
The Moray See You
Yabby Road
There's a Storm Across the Trevally
Old Dogs and Children and Watermelon Tarwhine
Love Is a Many Splendoured Ling
Eel Have To Go
Kippery Doo Da, Kippery Ay
Tell Him That You've Never Gurnard Leave Him

♪♫♩♪ Ling Went the Strings of My Carp ♪♫♩

If You Knew Sushi Like I Know Sushi
Ling Went the Strings of My Carp
Sharkin' All Over
Oh Me Marlin Clementine
Duelling Banjo Sharks
Somebody Sole My Gal
Crabba Dabba Honeymoon

Most popular composers: Simon and Garfish and Rodgers and Hammerhead.
Most popular group: The Trevallying Wilberries.
Most popular singers: Pike and Tina Tuna and Shirley Wrassey.

So the next time you're out fishing with your mates and the bites are as scarce as feathers on a frog, have a crack at the Fish Hit Parade and you'll keep yourselves in stitches all day.

Crocodile Boots

*I've met some dopes in fishing over the years, but Merv
'Crayfish' Gibbons takes the cake. He was a real dill.
Long and lean, Crayfish wore a bushie's hat and boots,
making his country background a dead giveaway.
They reckoned that when he pulled his zipper down for a
slash, every sheep within 5 kilometres would hide.*

Crayfish started off fishing the rivers and creeks around Gippsland but moved to Sydney to chase a bit of tail around Kings Cross. He must've found a bit, 'cos he stayed — much to the ongoing torment of us poor devils at the fishing club.

He thought we called him Crayfish because he loved bottom fishing. You know, around the reefy cave areas. Truth is, it was because he was all arms and legs and had a head full of shit. That was him to a tee.

One day Crayfish announced that he was taking a holiday in Darwin. We breathed a sigh of relief — we'd have a bit of peace for a couple of weeks. He had teamed up with the other club idiot, Alf 'Rust' Timms, and between them they had saved enough to bunk at a cheap hotel, do a bit of fishing and stay drunk the whole time.

They shopped around and got a great deal, for about half the normal price. Actually, we thought they had done something smart until we found out that they had booked in January – right in the middle of the cyclone season. Nobody bothered to tell them, for fear they would change their minds.

The story goes that they arrived in the middle of a decent gale and spent the first week lashed to the bar of the pub. As the winds subsided they decided to do a bit of shopping.

Rust – we called him that because once he got into your boat it was impossible to get him out – walked ahead while Crayfish dawdled along looking in the shop windows.

'Hey Rust,' Crayfish yelled, 'come and have a look at these.'

There in the boot shop, at the end of the aisle and with a dozen spotlights on them, was the most magnificent pair of boots Crayfish had ever seen in his life.

He was mesmerised. The heels were Cuban, the sides were buckled and the toes were capped with shining gold metal. But it was the leather which captivated our hero.

'Struth, Rust, I've never seen anything like that before in my life. What is it?'

'They're crocodile boots, mate,' informed Rust.

Crayfish had to have them. 'How much are the boots?' he asked the store attendant.

The salesman looked him up and down, noting the thongs, huge beer gut and the 'Life. Be In It' T-shirt, and wasn't wrong when he said, 'They may be a little out of your league, sir. About $1500 and they're yours.'

Crayfish's heart sank. Rust grabbed him by the sleeve and dragged him outside.

'You liked them, didn't you?' asked Rust.

'Sure did,' came the whimpering reply.

'Well, you can't afford to buy 'em, so why don't we get our own?' said Rust. Crayfish was confused. 'Whadda ya mean?'

'Do you realise where we are?' said Rust.

'Of course I do,' said Crayfish, logic working overtime. 'We're in Darwin.'

'And do you know what Darwin's famous for? Don't bother. Let me

tell you – crocodiles! There's millions of the bastards. They swim down from Borneo to get here. They eat the tourists. They nick kids out of prams. Next they'll be crawling down the main street. Let's get our own crocodile boots.'

Crayfish was still confused. 'How?'

'Simple,' said his mate. 'We'll rent two boats and go in different directions on one of the main creeks. That way we'll be sure to find a croc.'

And so off they went. Rust chose the northern channel. No matter how hard he searched, he couldn't find a croc anywhere.

Back at the boat hire shop, he waited in vain for Crayfish.

'You'd better go and have a look for your mate,' the boat man suggested. 'He's an hour overdue – and he's such a dill anything could have happened to him.'

Rust headed down the south channel, and as he rounded the first corner he nearly ran over a 5 metre crocodile, lying on its back, gasping its final breath.

Close inspection revealed that its neck had been broken.

'My God,' he thought. 'Poor Crayfish ... I hope he's OK!'

Further down the creek he rounded another bend and came across an even bigger croc – as dead as a doornail. Not only was its neck broken, but all its legs were fractured and its huge tail was bent at a right angle.

Rust was by now hysterical with worry. He sped down the creek calling for his mate. As he rounded a long bend he came across the most bizarre sight.

There was Crayfish with an Indian deathlock on a 6 metre giant croc! The reptile's jaws were snapping and snarling and froth was spurting from its nostrils.

Rust couldn't believe his eyes. Crayfish spotted him out of the corner of his eye. 'G'day mate,' he yelled.

'Are you all right,' called Rust.

'Yeah, for the moment.'

'Need a hand?'

'No, not right now,' puffed Crayfish. 'But if this bastard hasn't got any boots on, I'm goin' back to the pub for a beer!'

The Bottle Shop Bargain

Swap a fish for a case of beer? No problem. I thought I'd got a really good deal. But it didn't quite work out that way.

The bloke at the local grog shop had been robbing me for years. But it suited me to go there, even though I knew I was paying five bucks more for a carton of beer than I would at the discounters. I could park right out the front – and he was always good for a chat.

Over the years I could have saved a fortune by going elsewhere, but we had become good mates and the money wasn't all that important.

I'd never really thought about getting even with him until a while back. My young bloke Ben and I had just returned from a long day's fishing off Sydney and we called in for a carton of ice-colds on the way home.

'Been fishin', boys?' the old burglar asked us. 'You look as though you might have caught something.'

We had. But not what we wanted. We had gone out on a charter boat hoping to get big yellowfin and albacore tuna, but all we had managed to catch was a boatload of striped tuna – skipjack tuna, as they are known in some states.

The stripeys were up around the 5 kilogram mark, and great fun to catch on 3 kilogram and 6 kilogram line, but they are a blood tuna, and have rich, red flesh which is lousy to eat, not like the delicious pink-fleshed albacore and yellowfin tuna.

As I'd promised about 500 people some tuna steaks, it had been a disappointing day.

Not all tuna are good eating, and on a scale of 1 to 10, the poor old stripey would pull a zero. However, the Greeks and Italians love it, because they know how to marinate and cook it in oil and spices and disguise the rich, bloody flavour.

Anyway, back to the plot. As disappointed as we were at not catching some eating fish, I had still snookered a couple of good-sized stripeys for our three cats. They loved it – these fish would save me a fortune in canned food over the next week or so.

Besides, I love the way the cats react when I plonk a whole tuna across their bowl. They flick their tails and parade around the poor old stripey, taking jabs at it with their claws before they tear bits off it and start to eat. It's sort of a moggy ritual.

So when my thieving friend at the bottle shop inquired as to the day's results I casually answered … 'Yeah. We didn't do too bad. Just a whole heap of tuna.'

'Tuna!' he exclaimed. 'You're kidding. My wife loves tuna.'

I stopped dead in my tracks. The only tuna he would ever have had would be the white-fleshed variety. He assumed all tuna tasted the same. And to him they all *looked* the same.

I decided to do him a deal on the stripey. And if he started to grizzle and whinge later on that it tasted lousy and made his kids crook, I would say it must have been the way he cooked it.

I explained that I had only brought a couple home and they were promised. By now he was pleading.

I winked at Ben, who joined me in the con, begging me not to give any away on the pretext that he wanted to show his mates what he had caught.

'Besides,' I lied, 'they're $20 a kilo at the markets at the moment.' I knew full well that he wouldn't know it was the yellowfin and albacore that were bringing in the big bucks. If stripey ever made it to the markets it would be lucky to bring a dollar a kilo.

'I'll swap you a case of beer for one,' he said, tumbling into us at a million miles an hour. We had him.

'No, Dad,' Ben protested. 'They're my fish. I caught them. You can't do it to me.'

The more distressed my kid looked, the more determined the old shafter became to get one of those tuna.

Brushing Ben aside, I begrudgingly swapped the stripey for a case of beer, assuring him all the time that he had come out on top.

Young Ben was really proud of his catch and didn't want to swap it for a case of beer.

Ben's whingeing turned to shrieks of laughter as we walked out of earshot with our free case of beer.

'Got him,' I said to my son. 'I can't wait to see the look on his face when he tells us what it tasted like.'

The following day curiosity got the better of us and we fronted up at the liquor store.

'How was the fish?' I enquired. 'I haven't had it yet,' he said. 'My wife is preparing it for tonight – we're having some friends over for a barbecue.'

Yuk. Barbecued stripey. What a horrible thought. I nearly threw up. And he was going to feed it to his friends!

I felt like warning him, but the joke had gone too far. The next day curiosity got the better of us again.

Half expecting him to hit me over the head with an empty wine bottle for embarrassing him and his family in front of their toffy friends who had come over for a whoop-up tuna treat, I asked: 'How was the fish?'

'It was sensational,' he said. 'Best bit of fish we've ever eaten. I'll take as many of those as you can catch.'

I was dumbfounded. No one could eat stripey and enjoy it. Except my greedy cats.

Admittedly, I had my case of beer and I was a mile in front, but my joke had backfired.

Maybe I had been wrong about stripeys.

Out of curiosity we barbecued some of the other one we had at home. It was bloody awful.

A week later I called in to the bottle-o again. The old scoundrel was not to be seen.

'Dad's on holiday,' his daughter told me.

I couldn't help myself. 'Did you really enjoy that fish?' I asked, desperate to know.

'You mean that tuna?' she replied. 'Hell no. Dad didn't eat it – he sold it to the Italian guy next door for $80. He hasn't stopped laughing since.'

My Hero – Bob Dyer

*All boys have heroes, and mine was the late and great
Bob Dyer. But unlike most other kids, I was fortunate
enough to meet and even fish with my hero, who left an
indelible impression on my fishing career and my life.*

My childhood hero was Bob Dyer. That was back in the 1950s
and 1960s, when Bob ruled Australian radio and TV –
his *Pick A Box* was about the biggest quiz show ever to hit
this country.

But while I admired Bob's on-air antics, it was his ability with a
fishing rod and reel that really endeared him to me. I kept all the press
clippings about his giant catches, was mesmerised by the newsreel
footage and wished that one day I could be just like him and roam the
waterways of the world in search of giant sea creatures.

Bob's best publicity came from the huge catches of sharks that he
took out of Brisbane's Moreton Bay in the 1950s – he and his crew
would head out to Yellow Patch on a Friday night in his 11 metre
Tennessee and return late Sunday afternoon towing a dozen or so whalers,
tigers and white pointers for the public to gawk over.

And the sharks were huge: nothing was under 400 kilograms, and
some of the white pointers were as big as 1000 kilograms and 5 metres
long. The fans would gather in their thousands at the weigh station and

Bob made the most of it, hamming it up in front of the cameras and telling the adoring public tales of how the savage man-eating beasts had attacked the boat in a feeding frenzy and he and his crew had been lucky to escape with their lives.

That was back in the days when the world was ignorant; what we now know to be beautiful sea creatures — such as whales and sharks — were considered dangerous monsters that must be killed and put to man's best use.

On the way out to his chosen fishing ground, Bob would call in at the Moreton Bay whaling station and pick up as much whale oil, blood and blubber as his boat could carry. Once they were anchored up, the crew would berley with the whale offal and hundreds of sharks would cruise in for a snack.

Bob was a huge man, and contrary to popular belief, he was deadly serious about his fishing — he was also one of the world's truly great anglers. Having selected which shark he would like to catch, he would feed it a bait attached to a heavy wire trace, set the hook and the battle would rage — sometimes for many hours. But not all the sharks that were hooked were landed. One of Bob's crewmen, Jack Farrell, who I fished with many times in later years, told me amazing stories of breathtaking danger at the side of the boat.

'The big whites and the tigers were the worst,' Jack told me. 'It was all right for Bob to get all the glory at the weigh station, but it was us poor buggers on the gaffs and with the tail ropes that nearly got killed. The most awful trait of tigers and whites is that they roll up in the gaff ropes — sort of like a huge, snapping, aquatic yo-yo — and the more they twist and lunge in the ropes, the closer they get to actually coming into the boat with us.

'And don't ever let anyone tell you that sharks aren't agile and quick,' he went on. 'With their torsos and tails wrapped up in the ropes, their huge heads would appear from nowhere over the side and they'd come at us in mid-air, biting and growling and lunging at anything in their way. I nearly got my head bitten off a hundred times by sharks with mouths the size of 44 gallon drums. It was a living nightmare.

Bob says hello to a whopper white pointer caught off Moreton Bay in Queensland.

'A lot of those huge sharks were just too big to handle – they escaped by sheer brute force as they smashed the gaffs, ropes and the boat. We weighed a lot of world records, but every white pointer, tiger and whaler shark record in the world is still swimming around out there somewhere after having escaped from us.'

My friend Jack is gone now, and so is Bob; and, fortunately, so are those barbaric times when killing giant sea creatures was called adventure and the men who did it were called heroes. It was even legal way back then to harpoon dolphins and use them as berley and bait. This has long been outlawed, as has the use of mammal offal as berley and bait.

But back then we didn't see it as barbaric. To me, my hero, Bob Dyer, was a great man who just did what few other men were game to do but even fewer ever did.

As I grew older and my fishing preferences changed from beach fishing to rock fishing and then boat fishing, I eventually got to be a deckhand on a gamefishing boat out of Sydney, and one day at the Sydney Game Fishing Club I was introduced to Bob Dyer. I couldn't believe it. There I was shaking hands with the great man himself.

My skipper knew that I idolised Bob and said to him, 'Paul's our bilge rat. He's just started at the bottom in gamefishing, Bob. Have you got a bit of advice for him?'

My hero towered over me, squeezed my hand in his huge mitt and said, 'I certainly have, young fella. Always remember that a man's boat is his castle and that you are a guest. Always leave it as you find it. Scrub the decks hard and don't leave a trace of the day's activities. That way you'll always be welcome. Some day you will be welcome on my boat.'

Little did he realise just how true those words would be. I couldn't wait to get home that night to ring my mum in Perth and tell her I'd actually met Bob Dyer.

Through hard work and leaving people's boats as I found them, I eventually wound up as fishing master on Keith Whitehead's magnificent 11 metre Bertram, *Splashdown*. Keith was a three-time Olympian, having represented Australia in water polo. He was also a great friend of Bob Dyer – whom he called Pappy because Bob had grown a big white beard. We used to bump into Bob from time to time and I got to say hello, but of course he never remembered me and I never reminded him of our brief encounter.

Bob and Dolly Dyer with a pair of marlin taken off Sydney.

During all that time Bob never did or said anything to shatter my opinion of him. He was always the man I had imagined him to be. He was polite and charming with the ladies, never got drunk and disgraced himself, was humble, and was always in demand as an after-dinner speaker at gamefishing presentation nights. I was very proud that Bob Dyer had said hello to me; he was still my hero.

And then one day when we were having a lay-day on *Splashdown* at Greenwell Point, south of Sydney, and Bob Dyer's 16 metre *Blue Rhapsody* was tied up at the wharf beside us, Bob walked up to the bow of his boat and suggested to Keith that as he (Keith) wasn't going fishing that day, maybe the 'young bloke' might like to go out fishing with him (Bob) for the day.

Go fishing with Bob Dyer? I couldn't believe my ears, but it was true. I didn't have to be asked twice. And what a day it was. Bob caught and released a small marlin – on light tackle – and I got to see just what a great angler he was. And when the day was over and *Blue Rhapsody* was tied up at the wharf again, our team from *Splashdown* joined Bob and his crew for drinks. We all sat around and chatted, and encouraged Bob to talk about the old days.

And when he did talk of those bygone days when the men who went to sea to kill giant sea creatures were heroes to a nation, he spoke with much sadness and regret about having taken the lives of so many living things. He spoke of their gallantry in trying to escape, their terror as they lunged in the gaff ropes at his crew and their distress as they died a slow death tied up by their tails to the back of the boat.

He wondered if they felt humiliation as they were strung up on the gantry – the way murderers in the Dark Ages were – and said that really, their only crime was being hungry. In the last 15 years of his life, Bob Dyer never killed a living thing unless it was for the table.

He preached to others about the foolishness of wanton destruction of living creatures. And they listened. Now more than 90% of fish caught in gamefishing competitions, including sharks, are released to fight another day.

I am still very pleased that Bob Dyer was my hero.

Gaffer Bourke

Every sport, including fishing, has its unsung heroes.
Rodeos have the clowns, cross-country rallies have the
navigators, and fishing has the trace and gaff men and
women who carry out thankless and extremely dangerous
tasks. This story is about the greatest gaffer of them all
— it's a tribute to gaffers and tracers everywhere, and to
their heroic contribution to fishing.

In every critical situation there's a hero or a lunatic or a heroic lunatic — it depends on how you look at it. It would be fair to say that the engineers in the Vietnam War, the brave men who went ahead of the troops and searched for booby-trapped tunnels, were real heroes, putting their lives on the line daily.

And during the American Civil War, the brave, yet naively foolish soldiers, some as young as twelve, would huddle together on their opposite sides the night before a battle and help each other sew large numbers on the backs of their tunics so that their bodies could be identified the following day, when they would be killed, and their loved ones could be notified of their heroic deaths.

On the other hand, it could be said that the Japanese Kamikaze (which means 'divine wind') pilots of World War II, who flew their planes on suicide missions into the pride of the American navy to ensure themselves an easy ride into the next life, were complete fools.

Sorry, but even if you could convince me that Elle McPherson, Demi Moore, Cindy Crawford and Marilyn Monroe were waiting for me on the other side with Dom Perignon poured, Beluga caviar chilled and grapes peeled, I would still not fly my plane into the side of a battleship over a kilometre long with all its guns blazing at me.

The old story goes that the Kamikaze instructor informed the would-be pilots that they only had enough fuel to get out to the American fleet; when they got there they had to fly their planes into the biggest battleship they could find and kill themselves and as many Americans as they could for the glory of Japan.

He then asked if there were any questions, and a guy at the back called out, 'Are you *serious?*'

God or no God, to my mind that lot were complete dills. I have a list of ways I want to die, and believe me, flying a plane into a battleship isn't even in the first 25,000.

So there you have it, three examples and three different qualities: brave, foolishly brave, and completely foolish. Which leads me to my point – which, believe it or not, is about fishing heroes. Every self-respecting gamefishing boat that heads seaward requires the services of one or more persons with one or all of the above qualities.

That poor individual is known as the traceman or the gaffman/woman – or in cases of extreme lunacy, both; there are some individuals who can perform both of these skilful and extremely dangerous tasks.

These people, who clearly have scant regard for life or limb, are the last bastion between an angler and his fish after a battle that could have been raging for hours with a sea creature so huge that it defies the imagination of even Steven Spielberg.

It is these people's job to see to it that the huge marlin, sharks and tuna are brought to the side of the boat to be released, usually after an identifying tag has been stuck in them, or gaffed and killed and taken in to the weigh station to be admired or booed (the latter is becoming more fashionable these days) by the masses.

It's their job to grab hold of the wire or thick nylon trace (it can be up to 9 metres in length) which is attached to the lure or bait that the fish has eaten at one end and the angler's line at the other. In regulation gamefishing, where strict rules apply, a trace is allowed in order to prevent the fish from escaping by biting through the line or rolling in it and breaking it on its rough skin, teeth or beak. It also gives the traceman something decent to hang on to when he's bringing the fish, which is more often than not going berserk by now, close enough to the boat to get a gaff into it.

The brave, foolishly brave or just plain foolish individuals I know are Mako Bob, Gaffer Bourke, Great White Wally, Johnny Nine Fingers, Limbs Mackenzie and Fearless Syd (so named for obvious reasons), and each has many a tale to tell of death or of near-death experiences at the fins of mighty sea creatures – creatures they have been close enough to to smell the breath of.

You see, the easiest part of catching a giant fish is the actual angling itself. The person who sits in the chair and cranks the reel handle and pays the bills usually gets all the glory, but it's the skipper and crew who really do all the hard yards, particularly on charter vessels, where in most cases the paying customers wouldn't know the difference between a black marlin and Marlon Brando.

By far the most dangerous action is at the end of the battle, at the side of the boat, when the fish has to be traced and brought close enough to be either tagged and released or gaffed.

Tagging is hard and dangerous enough, but sticking giant flying gaff hooks – which are attached to ropes secured around the stem of the game chair – into huge sharks (especially white pointers, tigers and makos) or marlin is another thing again.

Noted Australian gamefishing author Peter Goadby is a member of one of the most exclusive clubs on Earth, 'The Underwater Traceman's Club', which you can only get to be a member of by being dragged over the side of the boat by a huge fish as you hang on to the trace. Goadby was dragged into the briny by a 500 kilogram plus black marlin, and thus joins the very select few who have survived to tell the tale.

I suspect that there are many other eligible members throughout the world but they are too embarrassed to come forward and claim membership.

But without a doubt, the most horrifying fishing experience is wiring or gaffing a big shark. Tigers and whites roll up in the trace and flying head gaff ropes, and makos jump clear of the water in an effort to break free.

Back in the old days when I used to kill sharks, I was almost killed myself when a 400 kilogram mako shark I gaffed jumped the entire length (5 metres) of the gaff rope and almost came into the boat. I recall it snapping and snarling about an inch from my face, and let me tell you, its breath was so vile it almost permed my hair. It landed on one of the other crewmen's hand on the skirting board, breaking it.

The late Jack Farrell used to tell me stories of huge white pointers and tiger sharks that would roll up in the traces and gaff ropes 'like a giant, aquatic yo-yo, Paul' he would say as I listened, spellbound. 'Bob [Dyer] would play a huge tiger or white pointer to the side of the boat and it was our job to trace, gaff and secure it to the boat so we could take it back to the weigh station for the spectators to look at.'

And while the tales of these heroic deeds of the sea are many, sadly, some are fatal. Overseas, a traceman took a couple of wraps on the wire as a small marlin of around 150 kilograms was played to the boat. Unfortunately, he got caught up in the trace – the marlin turned and headed for the depths, taking the traceman with it, and neither of them was seen again.

But the classic would have to be the legendary Sydney gaffman,

Gaffer Bourke.

Ray 'the Gaffer' Bourke, whom I crewed with on Keith Whitehead's *Splashdown* for donkey's years, and who performed some of the most extraordinary and fearless gaffing feats in the history of offshore angling.

The Gaffer was a big lump of a bloke who managed the Forbes Club, an illegal gambling casino in Kings Cross in the 1960s and 1970s. The Gaffer saw more action in a night than most folk would see in a dozen lifetimes, and when it came to a bit of bravado and biffo, the Gaffer was ready for anything … and that most certainly included ornery critters like marlin and sharks.

One of his favourite tricks was to gaff small marlin – up to 50–60 kilograms – in mid-air as they jumped on the trace at the back of the boat. The Gaffer would just reach out with a long-handled fixed-head gaff, anticipate where the fish was going to jump out of the water as the traceman (usually me) hung on for grim death, then just pluck the fish out of mid-air and into the boat.

To the Gaffer that was the end of his job. He'd grab a cold can of Resch's and piss off up onto the flying bridge with the skipper, leaving our lady deckie, Aileen Malone, and me with a very pissed off marlin going ape in the cockpit; then they'd abuse us for getting blood all over the boat. The blood was usually Aileen's or mine.

Another one of the Gaffer's tricks was to hang around the berley pot that was secured to the stern of the boat while we were berleying and drifting for sharks, gaff at the ready. If a mako of 50–60 kilograms came sniffing around the pot, the Gaffer would just reach out with the fixed-head gaff, drag the mako on board before it knew what had hit it and throw it at anyone who happened to be nearby.

If you've ever seen a little mako, gaffed and in a rotten mood, going ballistic and jumping around snapping its razor-sharp fangs into anything – including stainless steel, wood, iron, plastic and humans – you would know that being in a cockpit with one is not a good place to be.

One day the Gaffer chucked one that was about 40 kilograms on a poor innocent car dealer, Ray 'Snorks' Brown, who had just come along for the ride. The only sharks Snorks had ever seen before were the blokes he worked with. The Gaffer lobbed the mako at Snorks' feet. It bit him on the leg and then chased him around the cockpit for half an hour, snapping at him and smashing everything in sight with its tail.

The Gaffer thought it was great fun until Snorks, who was no spring chicken, clutched his heart – the skipper, Keith Whitehead, ordered the shark thrown out of the boat before we had a corpse on our hands.

But the classic of them all was the time when the Gaffer gaffed a marlin and there was no way that he could lift it into the boat. The Gaffer's legendary status had come about mainly because of his strength and bulk, which saw to it that he could lift any fish straight into the boat; other gaffmen of similar status would have to seek help. With the Gaffer it would be in with the gaff and straight into the cockpit, in one move. He was famous for it.

Mind you, these feats were performed off Sydney and Port Stephens (300 kilometres north of Sydney), and the black and striped marlin we caught back in those days rarely went more than 75 kilograms, which was well within the Gaffer's lifting capacity.

This day Aileen had played a very busy little black marlin of around 60 kilograms to the back of the boat. She moved back in the cockpit to allow the Gaffer to do his thing.

Whack! In went the gaff, with deadly accuracy, and the Gaffer pulled on the handle to drag the fish aboard. Nothing happened. The fish wouldn't budge. No matter how hard he tried, the Gaffer couldn't move the fish an inch.

He got terribly upset. His unblemished record was at stake! But no matter how hard he pulled, huffing and puffing, he couldn't budge that little marlin.

It was tragic to see the Gaffer give up. His reputation was in tatters. He was a broken man. He sat in the cockpit, head in his hands, weary, beaten by this mysterious fish. It was such a tragic moment that our skipper, Keith Whitehead, actually got off his big butt and came down from the flying bridge to console him. Aileen and I held on to the gaff and the fish that was still on the end of it, but concealed beneath the hull of the boat.

'I'm not sure, Gaffer,' Whitehead said, looking over the side at the fish, 'but I think your reputation as the world's best gaffer is still intact. In fact I think you've improved on it.'

The Gaffer looked up. 'Whadda ya mean?' he asked.

'No wonder you couldn't lift that fish. You gaffed it so hard that the gaff went straight through it and into the hull of the boat. No wonder it wouldn't budge. You've been trying to lift a 17 ton Bertram into its own cockpit!'

The Gaffer's reputation was intact – and it still is. There has never been and never will be another Gaffer Bourke. Some things aren't meant to be changed.

So here's to the legendary Gaffer Bourke and the other brave men and the occasional woman of his kind with limbs missing, nervous twitches, eye patches, scars and an obvious desire to be killed at sea.

They are truly the unsung heroes of fishing.

Gaffer Bourke died in December 2001. It was a great honour for me to be asked to give his eulogy. In it I included the story of his greatest gaffing feat, as told here. It brought the house down. As a parting gesture to a good friend and a great bloke, the congregation stood and gave him a final round of applause.

Political Correctness in Fishing

Skipjill tuna? Alicebacores? Queen Georgina whiting?
Sting Raelenes? Could these become the names of fish in
the future? Or has the old fishing scribe gone around the
twist? No he hasn't, but if the public servants who chew
up our taxes in pursuit of something to do have anything
to do with it, this could well be the case.

What I'm talking about is 'political correctness', the modern terminology for what we used to know as 'absolute stupidity', which is all the go these days. I guess it's only a matter of time before some wombat inflicts it on us poor fishos and believe me, the day that happens is going to be a very sad day for fishing in this country.

Not that any of us will take any notice of it, of course, because after all, the reason we go fishing is to get away from all the rules and regulations of everyday living and relax and catch a fish.

But, fellow anglers, it's going to happen. Some billygoat in the safe employ of the government will come up with a few suggestions for how we should curb our tongues for the better good of all. After all, the bureaucrats look upon us fishos as a crude lot anyway.

Political correctness in fishing started a few years back, when the then

Federal Minister for Resources, Mr Beddall, announced name changes to some fish so that they would be known uniformly throughout the country.

Redfish reverted to its correct name of nannygai, dolphin fish became mahi-mahi (so that non-fisherfolk would stop thinking that we were killing Flipper), and we were no longer allowed to refer to the blackfish or luderick by the highly reprehensible name of 'nigger'. Good stuff. All perfectly understandable in helping us recognise our fish from state to state.

Will this skipjack tuna become a skipjill tuna?

That's the type of political correctness that I like. Stuff that's made up of commonsense and logic. Any government body that improves our fishing jargon nationally and gives uniformity to the species is right up my alley.

But it's the lunatic fringe in this new political correctness that worries me. You know exactly what I mean. At one stage some of the airheads were so politically correct that they were going to change 'man' hole covers to 'person' hole covers so as not to offend anyone.

These days, in my columns and articles I find myself too afraid to refer to my brethren as 'fishermen'. According to political correctness they must be fisherfolk or anglers unless in the particular instance that I am writing about they are men.

An editor friend of mine tells me that it is politically incorrect to refer to boats as 'she' because it discriminates against women. I disagree. After all, when a ship is launched, doesn't it instinctively head for the 'buoys'?

Apparently it is politically incorrect these days to refer to Mother Nature as 'she', because it could be taken as offensive. Stupid, isn't it? I believe that it's out of hand in our society, and I wonder just how far it's going to go, especially in fishing.

If it does get out of hand, the females of certain species are almost certainly in for a name change. Female mangrove jacks will become womangrove Jills, kingfish will become queenfish and vice versa, lady albacores will become Alicebacores, King George whiting will become Queen Georgina whiting, a sting ray will become a sting Raelene and a tailor will become a seamstress.

And would a Samson fish become a Delilah fish, king prawns become queen prawns, red emperor become red empresses and skipjack tuna become skipjill tuna? I mean, where would this all end?

A future conversation down at the fishing club could go something like this: 'Gee, we got into the seamstresses today, Bert. There was a giant school of 'em off Itley (formerly Manly). There were a few personrings (formerly herrings) in with 'em but they were being chased by the grey orderly sharks (formerly grey nurse sharks), and we did well until we ran into some visually impaired mullet (formerly blind mullet) at the Bondi treatment works.'

Or in a restaurant: 'We'll have the Itdory (formerly John Dory) fillets for the missus, some royal prawns (formerly king prawns) and grilled indigenous-fish fillets (formerly blackfish) for the kids, and I'll have some of the grilled Zionist-persuasion fish (formerly jewfish) cutlets, thanks.'

Oh boy, haven't we got a wonderful time ahead if the lunatic fringe gets its way! Maori wrasse will become indigenous New Zealander wrasse, baldchin

Will this mangrove jack become a woman-grove jill?

groper will become folically challenged-chin groper, trevally will become personally, billfish will become personfish, longtom will become longperson and tommy rough will become person rough.

Nannygai will become child-mindergai, while the dwarf spotted rock cod will become the vertically challenged spotted rock cod.

And so it goes on. Confused? Of course you are. Is it any wonder? And if you think fishing is a worry, what about when they bring the hammer down on the boats on our waterways that have such dubious handles as 'She Got The House', 'Sheila the Peeler' and 'Satan's Lady'.

Ouch! Won't the wowsers and do-gooders have a ball with them! Can't see 'em having much success, though, because if I know the boaties as well as I think I do, they'll whack 'em over the noggin with a Murray ... oops, sorry! ... a *person* cod.

Thirsty Bert

This is a true story and very much a part of Watsons Bay folklore. Sadly, the only folk who can verify it, Curly Lewis and Jack Farrell, are fishing in another place these days. But for few embellishments, this rendition is as close to the truth as I recall.

'Thirsty' Bert McRae loved a drink. Hence the nickname. Thirsty was the local pest at the Watsons Bay Hotel, the watering hole at the former fishing village inside Sydney's South Head.

Thirsty subsidised his unemployment benefits by freeloading drinks off tourists in exchange for stories about the locals and their fishing adventures, and the drunker Thirsty got, the louder, more raucous and bizarre the stories became.

'Come on, Thirsty, tell us another one,' the boggle-eyed tourists called as they plied him with more drink. The yarns would flow until he decided it was time to go home while he was still capable.

Home was Curly Lewis' 8 metre fishing boat *Gladys*, named after his fire-breathing old rock python of a wife and moored in the bay about 100 metres off the beach, right in front of Doyle's, the famous seafood restaurant.

Every night Thirsty had the Doyle's patrons in hysterics as he made his way home in his tiny dinghy – he would stand at the back, as full as a high-school hat-rack, rowing with the one central oar, like a Venetian gondolier, through the minefield of cabin cruisers and yachts that blocked his path.

This nightly spectacle was always best to watch in a raging southerly, when Thirsty would have the extra task of fending off boats as they swung dangerously on their moorings. Incredibly, he always made it. When he'd got home he'd crash in his bunk and snore and fart until Curly arrived at around 2 am, when they'd head out to fish the inshore reefs for snapper and jewfish.

Curly and Thirsty had formed this amicable fishing partnership years earlier, and it suited them both down to the ground. It gave Curly a chance to get away from the old death adder and provided Thirsty with a home and plenty of fishing, which was his favourite pastime – apart from getting pissed.

One night Thirsty had really done a job on himself. A busload of Yanks had hit the Bay at about 10 am and gathered Thirsty in tow. He'd entertained them all day, and in return they'd fed him and kept the whisky and beer flowing until he could take no more.

At about eight o'clock he made the evening pilgrimage out to *Gladys* and passed out on the cockpit floor, rotten. When Curly arrived at 2 am loaded up with food, bait and a bottle of rum, Thirsty was just recovering from the day's events, and was ready for the start of Round 2.

Curly fired up the noisy single diesel engine and off they went, Curly at the wheel and Thirsty sitting on the transom swigging on the bottle of rum with his feet hanging over the back.

The sea was as flat as a night carter's hat as *Gladys* headed east in search of fish. The roaring of the big Gardener diesel engine didn't allow for much chat ... but who cared? Curly just steered and looked into the blackness ahead, wafting off from time to time into his fantasy world of giant snapper and jewfish big enough to swallow a man whole.

Thirsty might be the world's greatest lush, he thought, but he was great company and a terrific fisherman. Life was great.

Curly didn't notice Thirsty fall overboard. Rendered unconscious by the repeated swigs of raw rum, Thirsty had gone to sleep sitting on the tuck of the boat and then fallen in.

By the time Thirsty realised what had happened, *Gladys* had disappeared into the night, the roaring engine noise removing any possibility of Curly hearing his cries for help.

Curly just kept steering ahead, oblivious to the disaster in his wake. Thirsty sobered up in an instant and coughed up a gallon of salt water from his lungs. He knew he was in deep shit.

'Fuckin' hell,' he thought. 'What do I do now?'

It was too far to swim home, and the chance of a passing boat finding him in the dark was remote. He trod water and assessed his situation. A lifetime at sea had taught him many things.

He knew that at this time of the year the warm currents ran from the north at around 1 knot. He also knew that the teraglin were on the bite at The Wreck – a popular reef about 3 kilometres south – so there was bound to be someone fishing there. He figured that if he just lay on his back and drifted with the current he should bump into one of the fishing boats in about four or five hours.

'Sharks won't be a problem,' he chuckled to himself. 'I'll just breathe on the poor bastards.'

And so Thirsty Bert floated south on his back – and into Watsons Bay folklore – at about 1 knot an hour, along the way collecting large clumps of floating seaweed to add to his buoyancy.

He was having a little nap when, about three hours later, he bumped into a moored vessel occupied by Mad Ivan the Russian, who was busy filling the boat with teraglin. The last thing Ivan was expecting was a guest.

Though he had lost much else in those years of alcohol-induced haze, Thirsty had not lost his manners. Rather than clamber aboard someone else's boat unannounced, he knocked on the hull, just as he would knock on someone's front door.

Mad Ivan almost shit himself. Armed with a boat-hook, he proceeded to attack the seaweed-encrusted sea monster clinging to the side of his

boat, until it spoke: "Scuse me, mate, you wouldn't happen to be going anywhere near Watsons Bay, would you?'

Hauled aboard, Thirsty had his new-found friend in hysterics within minutes, telling him that he was a perfectly harmless drunk who got his kicks out of floating around in the ocean at 6 am impersonating King Neptune.

Thirsty and Mad Ivan settled into a couple of bottles of vodka, caught heaps more teraglin and headed for home just after daybreak, only to run into the water police, who had responded to Curly's 'man overboard' call and were searching the area where he thought his mate had fallen in.

Thirsty got his 15 minutes of fame and lapped it up. The press had a ball with him.

But the novelty wore off the day he threw up all over Mike Walsh on *The Midday Show* while telling the story for the millionth time.

He enjoyed the limelight so much that a couple of years later he tried the same stunt again.

Whether it was fair dinkum or staged, no one will ever know, but this time he really did disappear – and he has never been seen since.

Is Fishing Cruel?

Is recreational fishing cruel? Do fish feel pain? Should certain forms of fishing be outlawed? Do fish feel fear? Do fish have emotions?

Yes, to all of the above, according to Australian Animal Liberation (AAL). In an article in the AAL newsletter not so long ago, Professor Bill Runciman, of the University of Adelaide said, 'Fish constitute the greatest source of confused thinking and inconsistency on Earth at the moment with respect to pain. You will get people very excited about dolphins because they are mammals, and about horses and dogs, if they are not treated properly. At the same time you will have fishing competitions on the river Murray at which thousands of people snare fish with hooks and allow them to asphyxiate on the banks, which is a fairly uncomfortable and miserable death. Once out of the water, fish suffocate like we do underwater. In their death throes fish writhe, gasping and flapping their gills as they desperately try to get oxygen. Anyone who has ever been unable to breathe even for a short time won't need convincing that this is a terrifying experience.'

I couldn't agree more. I think allowing a fish to die by suffocation is despicable. If you intend to take the fish home for the table, let it die with a bit of dignity. Kill it quickly. Cut its throat or break its neck. It is both humane and practical. Besides, fish taste a lot better when bled

immediately on capture. And if you don't intend to eat it, let it live and throw it back.

But some of the other claims by the AAL are not so cut and dried. They tell us that fish have the same nerve endings as humans and can therefore feel pain. They also tell us that a fishing hook embedded in a fish's mouth and the constant pressure from an angler's line when hooked causes the fish great pain and stress.

This is where AAL and I part ways. If the needle point of a fish hook embedded in a fish's mouth causes such great pain, how do fish get on when they eat other fish that are covered in more spikes and pricks than you'd find in a dozen aloe vera cactus farms?

And how does the humble bream survive the pain after it has supped on oysters which it got hold of by crushing their shells open with its powerful jaws? Haven't you ever chewed on a bit of oyster shell in a restaurant, the legacy of a dozen natural, kilpatrick or mornay? Of course you have. Well, imagine a mouthful of them. It would be like munching on a packet of razor blades, but bream do it every time they have a feed of oysters. So much for the pain of a single, needle-sharp fisherman's hook.

And I wonder how much agony a groper goes through when it's grazing on red rock crabs, its favourite tucker, and crunching on their shells and claws?

And you don't need me to tell you that crunching mussels up in your gob would be about as palatable as munching on a Swiss Army knife with all of its attachments at half-mast. But trevally, snapper, kingfish and every other recreational species do it all day every day.

And if you've ever fished for critters called black or silver drummers, you'd know that their favourite tucker is cunje, a meaty morsel found inside a shell that has edges like a bucket full of broken glass. The drummer has to get to the juicy meat inside, and the only way it can do that is to crunch on the shell. That's about the same as a fish having about 10,000 fish hooks in its mouth all at once.

So do fish feel the pain of the hook? I don't think so. We've hooked fish and let them go still attached to the line and with the hook in their mouths, and they've gone about their business as though nothing has happened.

We've caught the same kingfish 10 times in one day when we've had a school of them in the berley at the back of the boat. Bob Dyer had sharks eat their *own* entrails after they had been hooked, played, landed, cut open and thrown back in the water.

No, I don't believe that fish feel the pain of the hook. And it is definitely not the hook in their mouths that makes them resist the angler and put up a fight. It is disorientation, caused by not being able to go where they want to go. When they want to go in one direction and the angler is trying to pull them in another, they do what comes naturally, just like a bull does when a cowboy throws a lasso around its neck or a horse does when someone sits on its back for the first time.

Marlin, salmon, tailor, trout, sailfish, mahi-mahi, barramundi and mako sharks jump out of the water; groper, kingfish and drummer head back to the cave they just came out of; tiger sharks and yellowfin tuna bog down into the current; and Murray cod sit on the bottom and sulk. All species have their own distinct fighting characteristics.

Fish don't have the ability to reason when they are hooked – their brains are minuscule compared with their size (a 500 kilogram black marlin has a brain the size of a walnut) – so when they feel the resistance of the line, instinct tells them that all is not right and they do whatever is characteristic to their species.

The ocean is just one very big food chain. Everything in the sea eventually gets eaten by something else. The huge schools of slimy mackerel, yellowtail, pilchards, garfish, trigger fish and mullet serve no purpose other than to be eaten by other fish.

And the predators that eat them are eventually eaten by other fish, which eventually die and get eaten by the smaller fish, which are then eaten by bigger fish, and so it goes on.

The AAL also has a lot to say about the trauma that marlin go through being caught by big-game anglers. Absolute rubbish! Marlin have been hooked, fought, then tagged with a scientific recording tag and released, only to be caught again a few days, weeks or years later.

So much for being traumatised and having to visit the fish psychiatrist after being captured and released.

The AAL also vehemently opposes the use of live baiting – fishing for big predators by using a live fish as bait. They say that it is cruel and traumatising.

To my mind it is simply speeding up the inevitable. Baitfish are going to get eaten sooner or later; that's why they are in the oceans. As the baitfish have no ability to work out what is going on, and don't seem to show any effects of having a hook stuck through their shoulders or noses (and I would know, I've live-baited a thousand times), it seems to me a perfectly acceptable method of fishing and definitely not cruel. If it were a horse or a cat or dog, it would be cruel. But these are baitfish, not domestic pets. Besides, live cats and dogs are no good as shark bait because they always swim back to the boat and try to get back on board. Just kidding!

And these days live-baiting is not as widely spread a practice as the AAL would have us believe. Live-baiting the bottom for kingfish has been largely replaced by jigging with artificial lures, most marlin trolling is done with dead baits and lures, live-baiting for yellowfin tuna has been proved to be nowhere near as effective as cubing with dead pilchards, and live-baiting from the rocks for gamefish is nowhere near as popular as it was a few years back.

That aside, we must never lose sight of the fact that with the exception of the fish at the top of the food chain, such as sharks and marlin, almost everything else spends its entire life looking over its shoulder, wondering what's going to eat it.

This whopper barramundi is the catch of a lifetime. But is catching them cruel to the fish?

The timid bream, for instance, bites better on the dark of the moon, because when the moon's out and the predators can see better it runs a much bigger risk of being eaten, so it stays at home in the darkness and safety of its oyster lease or rock ledge.

Seems to me that a chiropractor would make a better living in the fish world than a psychiatrist – I'm sure there are more fish with crook necks than there are fish that are traumatised.

The other thing that AAL seems to conveniently forget is that recreational angling in Australia leads the world in letting fish go to fight another day, thanks to Rex Hunt's kiss-and-release concept and the tag-and-release program.

And judging by the number of tags that are recovered, fish seem to get over their stress, trauma and pain pretty quickly … if there is in fact anything to get over.

So apart from their views on fish suffocating to death, I think the animal liberationists should stay away from recreational fishing, because they simply don't know what they are talking about.

The Duck, The Chemist and Billy the Pig

Some fish fight better than others, and everyone
who dangles a line has their own preference.
But some species are just so darn ornery that tales of
their capture, or at least of the attempts at their
capture, are fishing folklore around the world.
Here are a couple of the best.

Ask any of the boys at the fishing club what's the best fighting fish in the world, and if there are 10 blokes there, they'll give you 10 different answers. There's certainly no outright winner.

Legendary American fishing and western writer Zane Grey was always in awe of the broadbill swordfish – the 'broadsworded gladiator' as he called it. He caught many in his long and illustrious career, but one of his stories will always stick out in my mind.

Fishing at Santa Catalina, off California, Grey elected to put his brother, Red, onto a broadbill. They hooked a fish of good size and the battle raged for three hours, until Red could fight the fish no longer.

Grey's boatman, the legendary Captain Laurie Mitchell, was ushered to the fighting chair. Mitchell was no slouch on the rod – he was the then black marlin world record holder.

Although they were aware that a second angler taking the rod disqualified the fish from any record claim, they still fought on for the sheer sport of having such a mighty fighting fish on the end of the line.

After four hours in the fighting chair Mitchell too had to concede defeat. The huge fish had beaten him to a standstill. In the gathering dusk Zane Grey, considered at the time the greatest angler in the world, took the chair and lay into the greenheart rod with fresh vigour.

The battle raged on into the night. For two hours the master angler pumped and wound, gaining line at every opportunity and giving it back equally as the fish showed no signs of giving in.

Then the strangest thing happened. Although they couldn't see far into the darkness, in the dead calm distance they could hear splashing noises. Then line would peel from the reel, followed by a much larger splashing noise and then silence. Then there would be the same small splashing noises again and another spasmodic burst of line from the reel and another large splash.

Grey was mystified. The gallant fish was jumping from the water in short bursts. But in a bid to escape? If the fish was so tired, surely they would have boated it by now?

Then it dawned on Grey what was happening. The small splashing noises were flying fish re-entering the water after jumping; the broadbill was feeding on them.

After nine hours of constant pressure on heavy gear, the fish had started feeding, as though it had never been hooked. It was chasing and pouncing on the flying fish, as fresh as the moment the battle started.

In disbelief, and probably out of respect, Grey cut the line and headed for home in the dark.

Having never caught a broadbill, or for that matter ever even hooked one, I must choose my toughest fighters from less exotic species. To my mind, yellowfin tuna, giant trevally, whaler sharks, bonefish and kingfish all rate among the top fighters.

But if you asked a long time ago mate of mine, Peter 'the Duck' King, what he regarded as the toughest fish in the ocean, he would have told you black drummer – more commonly known as pigs because of their dirty fighting habits.

Like kingfish and southern Australian blue groper, pigs are filthy fighters. They delight in grabbing a bait and heading straight back into their cave with it. And if it just so happens to have your hook in it, it's an instant bust-up. Goodnight Dick.

But pigs don't do this because they know there's a very sharp hook inside the morsel they have just mouthed. Oh no! And they haven't figured out that if they run your line over the rocks and barnacles at the entrance to their cave they will bust you off. No way.

That's the stuff rocket scientists are made of, and a drummer, or any fish for that matter, could hardly be classified as a candidate for Mensa. Besides, if they were that smart, they wouldn't take your bait in the first place.

No, they just duck out of their cave or apartment beneath a ledge, grab what's on offer, and duck back in the front door as quickly as they can so that they don't get mugged by another drummer trying to take the morsel from them. If your line happens to be attached to it ... stiff cheddar. You're busted.

It's as simple as that. Believe me, there are no table manners in Fishville.

So obviously the best tactic with an ambush fighter like the pig is to sink the hook quickly and hang on for grim death, hoping to turn the fish's head and at least get it coming your way before it can get back inside its front door.

These same tactics apply equally to other notorious ambush feeders, such as the legendary New Guinea black bass and the giant kingfish that have taken up permanent territorial residence in the caves honeycombed along the rock ledges of Jervis Bay in southern New South Wales.

The Duck, an extremely tough ex-front row rugby union player and equally tough plain-clothes detective, thought we called him by his nickname because his abbreviated name was P. King, as in Peking duck, the tasty Chinese dish.

He was such a tough bastard that we let him go on thinking like that.

But it was really because he spoke with a savage speech impediment, replacing his Rs with Ws. And what with being both a copper and a

A drummer, or 'pig', like this is a trophy for any rock fisherman. But Billy the Pig was a drummer big enough to break any rockhopper's heart

desperate rooter, he was always either trying to crack on to a sheila or crack a case he was working on.

'See that sheila over there? I'm gonna cwack on to her tonight,' he would say, his speech impediment working overtime.

Or, 'We're about to cwack that big jewellewy wobbewy in West Wyde.'

Or, 'I'll never forget the time we kwacked Wandwick's defence and I scored on the wight wing.'

Cwack, cwack. That's really why we called him the Duck. But no one was letting on.

The Duck had been fishing for pigs at this one secret spot at North Bondi for years, and had had great success with pigs of around 3–5 kilograms – a bit better than average size. But they came at a price.

All this time he had been having a running battle with the one giant resident pig, which had grown to enormous proportions thanks to his frequent berleying over the years with loaves of bread. The big pig and the Duck saw so much of each other that the Duck even had a name for his antagonist. He named it Billy, after the famous hotel in Bondi Junction, Billy the Pig's.

He had hooked that big old pig at least a dozen times, and each time Billy had smashed him up. Billy had caused the Duck enough headaches; he had to go.

So the Duck devised a plan. A two-man plan. And the other party had to be able to keep a secret, because the Duck didn't want anyone else to know his secret spot.

Such a person was the All Night Chemist, so named because he never shut up. The Chemist was a fanatical beach fisherman, and while he could talk underwater in an army overcoat with the pockets full of pennies, he was good with a secret, providing he was told that it was a secret and to keep his gob shut. The Chemist gave his word.

For two months before his planned assault on Billy the Pig, the Duck selected the juiciest and plumpest mussels and cabbage he could find, mixed it up with luscious Botany Bay weed with weevils in it and berleyed his spot like buggery.

But he didn't fish; he just berleyed, every day at precisely the same time. After a month Billy was well and truly conned, the memories of bygone battles long forgotten. At the end of six weeks Billy was on the surface, lying on his back in close with his gob open, waiting to be hand-fed. The Duck could almost reach out and pat it.

'Shitbrained fish,' he said to the Chemist. 'Now I'm gonna drive it nuts.' The Duck kept going to his secret spot every day for about a month, but now with no berley. Billy was waiting patiently for him, and when the Duck didn't feed him, the poor demented fish almost climbed up the rocks.

The Duck had Billy exactly where he wanted him. It was time to put the plan into action.

He had built a special rod for the occasion: it was a blank made out of the toughest space-age graphite in the world, and would load itself up like a pole vaulter's pole launching the jumper over the bar as soon as the fish grabbed the bait and headed for its cave.

The idea was that once the fish took off, the rod would only allow it to go so far. Then, bent to its limit, the rod would work the other way with a recoil so great that it would either turn the fish or (at worst) rip its head off.

For a reel he borrowed a huge gamefishing reel loaded with 130 pound breaking strain line that was normally used to catch giant black marlin at Cairns. He cranked the reversible drag up to the limit, ensuring that no matter what, the fish wasn't going to get one inch of line off that reel.

The Duck had also designed a special shoulder and back harness, complete with rod bucket and reel clips that attached him permanently to the rod and reel. Not unlike a man being strapped into the electric chair.

For his part, the Chemist's job was to stand behind the Duck, firmly hanging on to a length of rope that was attached to the harness – so the Duck wouldn't get dragged into the drink by the power of Billy the Pig in full retreat.

With all in readiness, the Duck fed Billy a huge, juicy piece of mussel meat, and when the big fish took off with it he leaned back into the rod and set the hook. The reaction was instant. Billy, sensing that something was dramatically wrong, headed for his cave at a million miles an hour, stretching the line to its limit and bending the rod almost to breaking point.

What happened next will never be known, but the general opinion is that Billy had a massive heart attack from obesity and died on the spot. And with suddenly no resistance from the fish, the Duck fell over backwards onto the Chemist as the recoil of the rod launched the giant pig into mid-air ... it reached the end of its tether, then rocketed earthwards and embedded itself into the Duck's face, as dead as a Randwick favourite.

The Chemist cracked up.

'Get this fuckin' thing off me,' the Duck begged, but try as he may, the Chemist could not lift the fish. He soon discovered why.

'Look at this!' he exclaimed. 'The old bastard's got about twenty hooks hangin' out of him from where he's been hooked all those times, and they've all embedded in your face. I can't cut 'em out and I can't pull 'em out. I'll have to take you to Emergency with the fish attached to you and they can get him off you.'

The Duck was in a bad way for a long time. His face was very cut up from the hooks and he ended up badly scarred. I didn't see much of him after that, but they tell me that some nights when the coppers all get together at the Bourbon and Beefsteak in Kings Cross for a few drinks, if you look closely at the Duck's face in the right light when he's pissed you can match the scars up and they read 'Billy'.

Fishing's Urban Myths

Being the pastime that it is, fishing is susceptible to more exaggerations and outright lies than all the other recreational activities combined. And I've heard them all at one stage or another. The most frightening part of it is that the tellers of these exaggerated out-of-all-proportion whoppers usually try to convince me that they were there when it happened, putting the story into the 'urban myth' category. Give me a break ...

An urban myth is a preposterous story told and retold so many times that the tellers not only end up believing it themselves, but try to convince anyone silly enough to listen that they were actually there when it happened.

Or, to a lesser degree, that their uncle, aunt, wife's brother or whoever told them the story was there when it happened. You must have heard an urban myth – like the woman who never washed her beehive hair-do and ended up with a nest of spiders living in it?

Or the woman who took her beloved French poodle into the Chinese restaurant and asked the staff to look after it while she had dinner? Only after the lady and her friends had finished their banquet and she went to collect Fifi did they find out that the dog was one of the exotic dishes they had just eaten.

And then there's the one about the bloke who was kissing and cuddling his girl at the drive-in when a gang of hoodlums picked up the back of his car and started bouncing it up and down. Starting the engine, he planted his foot to the floor, and the next time the wheels hit the ground he took off at a million miles an hour. When he got home he found a human arm, dripping blood, caught up in the bumper bar.

Anyone who would believe that crap would believe that Elvis was Jewish. But I can still see some readers saying, 'Dad, Paul B. Kidd reckons that that story you told us about Auntie Joan's first cousin's sister's boyfriend's next door neighbour's dog getting eaten in the Chinese restaurant is a load of crap.'

'Well, he doesn't know what he's talkin' about, son, because I was there and if I hadn't seen it with my own eyes, I wouldn't have believed it either.'

But he wasn't there and he didn't see it, because it didn't happen. It's all bullshit. It's an urban myth.

The trouble is, urban myths seem to badly afflict the fishing fraternity, too. Must be something to do with all the practice they get telling stories about the one that got away.

One such story is about a group of Tasmanians who went to Melbourne for a national fishing club convention. So familiar were these blokes with all the old jokes they regularly told each other that rather than repeat the details of the joke time and again, they had given them all numbers, and they would go into fits of laughter every time someone got up onto a chair and yelled 'Number 27', 'Number 23', and so on.

Told what was going on, the Melbourne club president couldn't believe it, so one of the Tasmanians invited him to have a go. Feeling like a fool, he stood on the chair and yelled; 'Number 66'.

All the Tasmanians fell about, laughing even harder than before. 'That brought the house down, didn't it?' the president said to the Tasmanian.

'Why wouldn't it?' he replied. 'We haven't heard it before.'

The fifty blokes I know who swear blind they were there that night and heard it are having themselves on. It didn't happen. It's an urban myth.

So is the one about the bloke who sought revenge on one of the meanest critters that swims and wound up regretting it in the worst possible way.

It's no secret that the huge kingfish at Jervis Bay, on the NSW south coast, are a bunch of pests. They live in the underwater caves that honeycomb the cliffs there, and often duck out to grab the rock-hoppers' catches as they are about to lift them from the water. Then it's straight back into the cave and goodnight to the anglers' catch and gear.

Our hero had lost hundreds of fish to them over the years, and figured that if he could hook one of these monsters on heavy enough gear and hang on, one of two things could happen: the line would break or he would catch the fish and teach it a lesson. So he bought a mammoth gamefishing reel and filled it up with 500 pound breaking strain line.

Then he strapped a huge game-fishing rod to himself with a harness that would normally be used for catching tiger sharks.

And so that he could hang on when the monster struck, he positioned himself in a chair-like structure among the rocks, bracing his feet against two large boulders about 20 metres from the rockface that disappeared into the underwater kingfish alley.

He got his mate to drop a live trevally on a 1000 pound trace into the water, pushed the drag on the reel up to beyond breaking point and hung on for grim death as the world's biggest kingfish

The Reverend Billy's first jewfish was a beauty, but it brought about his undoing.

shouldered about 50 of his mates out of the way, grabbed the trevally and headed back to his cave.

Until then, the theory was working just fine. But when the fish didn't give in and the line didn't break, things went drastically wrong. The slack took up as the kingie headed to his lounge room with his prize, and suddenly Boofhead was launched like a Patriot missile out of his rocky fighting chair and dragged screaming – on his face, elbows and knees – across the rocks to the cliff edge, where he, with his rod, reel and harness, disappeared like an Olympic high diver off the cliff and into the sea below.

All that remained to prove to the police that the carnage ever took place was some teeth, skin, a shoe, a broken reel handle and a bloodied path between the rocks. And search as they may, police divers found nothing.

True story? Absolutely, if you choose to believe at least four blokes I know who swear they were there when it happened. But they didn't see it, because it didn't happen. It's all bullshit. But they've told the story while holding court so many times that they actually believe it happened.

It's a fantasy ... an urban myth.

And then there's the all-time classic. Everyone's heard this beauty.

The Right Reverend Billy Goode had never been fishing before in his life, so when he caught a big jewfish, his first ever fish of any description, on a fishing outing on Sydney's Hawkesbury River with the over-60s' Born Again Christian Fishing Club, he thought it was a gift from above.

One can only try to imagine what a drab day's fishing it would be out with that lot of God-fearing wowsers. No bad language, no grog; only tea, and lots of 'Hallelujah, brother' and 'Praise the Lord'.

When the Reverend Billy turned up at home that night with the giant fish slung over his shoulder, Mrs Agnes Goode was beside herself with excitement and very proud of her husband's feat.

The following day she rang him at his office. 'Reverend,' she said, 'I have a special surprise for you when you come home tonight. I'll be waiting for you at the front door and I'm going to blindfold you and sit you down and then take off the blindfold and show you what it is.'

He couldn't wait. He half suspected that it would be a fabulous fish dinner, and sure enough, as he drove up the driveway to his home he copped the stunning aroma of freshly cooked fish. Once inside he went along with the charade and let his wife blindfold him and lead him into the dining room and sit him down.

'Just be patient,' she purred. 'I'll be back with the surprise in about five minutes. No peeking now.'

Mrs Goode had only been gone about a minute when the Reverend felt a giant fart coming on. It was a ripper. Probably those curried egg sandwiches I had for lunch, he thought.

He held off from letting it go for fear that Mrs Goode would come back into the room and catch him – then spend the rest of the night praying for his soul. But when it came on again, so badly that his stomach ached, he had to let it go.

'How long now, darling?' he called to the kitchen

'Only a couple more minutes,' she called back.

Anticipating that he was safe, the Reverend tilted his arse to just the right angle for maximum relief and let out the longest and loudest fart in a long and illustrious sneaky fart career. It was a ripper, and he chuckled to himself at the naughtiness of it all.

And it was off. Putrid, vile, sickening. 'I need pulling through with a knotted blanket,' he chuckled out loud to himself as he waved blindly in the air, desperately trying to disperse the stench before Mrs Goode returned with the surprise.

A few minutes later she entered the room and told him to take off the blindfold and get his surprise. It was as he had guessed – the whole baked jewfish, done in vegetables and ginger, and with slices of lemon all along the top.

But that wasn't the only surprise. Seated stoneyfaced at the huge dining table were the most prominent members of his congregation: the Lord and Lady Mayoress, the local school principal and her husband, the ladies from the Bible Society, the police chief and his wife, and assorted wowsers of all descriptions, all waiting in silence to surprise him, then congratulate him on his catch and share it with him.

Yes, it was a real surprise. So much so that the Right Reverend Billy Goode passed out from the shock of it all and applied for another posting the next day.

Another true story? Absolutely. How do I know? Because I was there. But then who's to say that this whole article isn't just one big urban myth?

Now that's got you thinking, hasn't it?

The Shark Arm Murder

*What started out as a day's fishing ended up as one
of the most bizarre murder mysteries the world
has known. Straight out of an Agatha Christie novel,
this extraordinary true story had the lot. A giant
shark, human body parts, shadowy suspects and another
grisly murder.*

Operators of Sydney's Coogee Aquarium, father and son Bert and Ron Hobson, couldn't believe their good fortune. They had had a very successful morning's fishing on 18 April 1935, with a captured 2 metre shark ready to be taken back to their exhibition, when a monster tiger shark cruised up, ate the smaller shark and became entangled in their net.

What a catch! The bigger shark would be a valuable attraction – much more so than the smaller fish. But from the minute it was released into the aquarium, the huge fish appeared to be off-colour and disoriented.

On Anzac Day, with quite a crowd gathered to view the latest exhibit, it shuddered and regurgitated the remains of a human arm, much to the horror of the onlookers. The police were called immediately.

Examination by police revealed that the arm carried a tattoo of two boxers 'shaping up' and had a length of rope tied around the wrist.

The tiger shark in Coogee Aquarium before it regurgitated the human arm.

Puzzled as to why the shark would vomit up the arm, authorities concluded that under normal circumstances the big shark would have digested it; it was obviously feeling a bit off-colour due to its new surroundings.

The shark proved this beyond doubt by dying five days later.

A post-mortem examination of the shark's stomach contents revealed nothing else that would help them with the case, and it was concluded that it was the smaller shark – the one this tiger shark had eaten – that had swallowed the arm in the first place.

But they didn't need a post-mortem to arrive at their other grisly conclusion: the arm had not been bitten off. Oh no! It was the work of a knife or a scalpel in the hands of a very inept surgeon.

An anatomy student perhaps? That line of investigation was quickly eliminated – there were two big slashes near the laceration, indicating extreme violence.

It seemed the body had been cut into bits and thrown into the sea to be eaten by the fish and become yet another unsolved 'missing persons' case. Who would have ever guessed that a shark would have brought up the evidence in an aquarium?

One can only wonder what the murderer must have thought when the story hit the headlines. What rotten luck for the killer.

The theories came thick and fast. One was that perhaps the arm had been preserved in formalin or some other kind of embalming fluid in a hospital for students to study. This theory was soon discounted when it was established that the arm had only been in the water a matter of days.

Another of the more plausible theories put forward was that it was the arm of an escaped mental patient whose body was found floating in Sydney Harbour … minus an arm. This story turned out to be a hoax.

But there was no escaping the fact that Sydney was in the grip of a murder most foul.

And while the scientists were trying to put the pieces together, so to speak, a woman identified the arm – through photographs in the paper – as that of her husband, 40-year-old James Smith, a Sydney billiards saloon manager, SP bookmaker and ex-employee of Sydney boatbuilder Reginald Holmes.

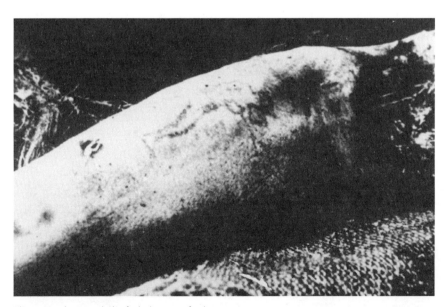

The severed arm with the faded tattoo of a boxer on it.

In the meantime, a well-known 42-year-old Sydney criminal and close associate of James Smith, a certain John Patrick Brady, was charged with the murder of Smith, on the grounds that he had recently visited the Sydney home of Reginald Holmes, who had recently had unsatisfactory business dealings with Smith.

Police instigated a mammoth search for the missing body parts around the Cronulla and Port Hacking districts – Brady had recently moved from a cottage in the district, taking with him a tin storage trunk, an anchor and two heavy window weights.

On 19 May, *The Truth* newspaper reported: 'Operating along the theory that the body might have been carved up, and perhaps only the arm with the identifying tattoo had been consigned to the waves, the police dug up certain premises, dragged the bottom of the bay, searched the tide-washed rocks, scoured the sandhills, but to no avail. The mystery is still as deep, and as apparently unsolvable as ever.'

Brady denied any involvement in the murder of Smith, and in his statement to police said that he had last seen the dead man with Holmes and another man.

Shortly after the police began a search for the elusive boatbuilder, there was another bizarre twist to the story. On the evening of 21 May, Sydney Water Police pursued a launch that was reported to be behaving in an erratic and dangerous fashion on Sydney Harbour.

During the ensuing four-hour chase, the wayward vessel attempted to ram the police launch four times before being apprehended. The driver turned out to be Reginald Holmes – he was dazed and had blood pouring from a gunshot wound to his head.

He claimed to have been fired upon, and said he believed the police were his clandestine attackers. Meanwhile, police took possession of a .32 calibre pistol from Holmes; they believed that the unstable Holmes had attempted to kill himself but had only grazed his head.

Holmes told detectives that Brady had murdered Smith and dumped his body, in a trunk, off Port Hacking. He also said that Brady had threatened his (Holmes') life if Holmes dobbed him in.

No charges were laid against Holmes and he was allowed to leave, on condition that he repeat this valuable information at an inquest into the death of James Smith.

Reginald Holmes never made it to the inquest. On 11 June, the day before the inquest was to begin, Holmes was found slumped over the steering wheel of his car, parked near the Sydney Harbour Bridge, with three bullets in his head. He had been shot at close range with a .32 calibre pistol.

John Patrick Brady was in police custody, charged with the murder of Smith, at the time of Holmes' murder.

At the inquest, a surprise witness turned out to be the wife of the recently deceased Holmes, Mrs Inie Parker-Holmes. She revealed her late husband's business dealings with Brady. Her husband had told her that Brady had confessed to killing Smith, placing the cut up body in a trunk and dumping it at sea.

A real estate agent, P.H. Forbes, identified Brady as the person who had rented a cottage from him under the name of 'Mr Williams' and then vacated the cottage, taking with him various items, including a tin trunk which had been replaced by a new and larger one.

Reginald Holmes, one of the main characters in the case, who was murdered the night before he was to face court.

John Patrick Brady was committed for trial for the murder of James Smith.

But the case was still shrouded in mystery. Persistent rumours involving underworld conspiracies, narcotics trafficking and organised crime dogged the trial, which was held before Mr Justice Jordan at the Central Criminal Court.

Brady admitted that on the night of 8 April he had accompanied Smith back to his (Brady's) cottage, but maintained that Smith had left in the company of well-known Sydney waterfront identities Albert Stannard and John Patrick Strong.

Brady was eventually acquitted because of insufficient evidence. He changed his name and dropped out of sight completely. Stannard and Strong were charged with the murder of Holmes. They were tried twice, but eventually were also acquitted.

And like all cases where fact makes fiction look ridiculous, there was one last twist to the tale.

In November 1952 a fire at the Holmes residence took the life of Mrs Inie Parker-Holmes.

The Fishermen Aren't Biting

Among the many stories that have become fishing folklore, this is one of the most famous, and there are many versions of it. This is the true story told in its entirety. Don't believe the other versions.

We christened him 'Spewie' because he was always going to 'bring it up' at the next meeting. Naturally, when his son was born we called him 'Chuck'. To this day I doubt that anyone knew their real names.

Spewie was a tally clerk on the wharves, and when Chuck was old enough to leave school he followed Dad and went to work on the docks.

They were inseparable, and as Chuck grew into manhood he'd join his old man at the pub a few times a week. They'd get as full as Dolly Parton's D-cups and make dreadful pests of themselves.

Their downfall was that they loved a stoush. They would fight anyone. Father and son would stand back to back and belt the shit out of anyone silly enough to stand up to them, then stagger over the pile of bleeding corpses and, arm-in-arm, sing their way home.

One night they met their match. They were pissed, as usual, and started giving a bad time to a couple of guys at the bar. It was a big mistake. They were bouncers from the illegal casino, and they were used to belting a dozen yobbos a night.

The thrashing was sickening. The bouncers broke every bone in Spewie and Chuck's bodies and kicked out every tooth in their heads.

When Spewie and Chuck got out of hospital, several months later, their fighting days were over. They decided on a far less dangerous pastime – fishing. They bought a half-cabin boat and spent afternoons and weekends in the harbour catching tailor, flathead, trevally and bream.

They could drink to their hearts' content and catch a feed into the bargain. Life was great.

After a while they became more adventurous, and ventured past the Heads and into the blue water in search of bigger fish.

It was only then that they discovered that Spewie was aptly named. Every time they went out wide of land he got crook. He simply couldn't help himself. Every fishing trip off the coast he would hang his head over the side and chunder.

Chuck would sympathise with his father by consoling him and taking care of his expensive dentures – full upper and lower, a legacy of 'that night', the night they never spoke about.

It was a pitiful sight. Dad over the side, gormless, going the giant up-and-under with his son standing dutifully behind him with a handful of bodgie choppers.

Over the years things got a little easier. At least Spewie wouldn't throw up on the way out. The minute the boat was moored up, though, he was off, head over the side and calling for his friends Ruuuth, Raaalph and Berrrt. But it was under control: once he had given in to the dreaded maldemer and emptied the contents of his stomach, he was OK. He would retrieve his fangs from Chuck, shoot 'em back in his gob, and they would settle down to a good day of fishing and drinking beer.

One day, however, Spewie was seriously crook. He'd had a skinful of the dreaded cask red wine the night before and the monumental hangover, combined with the engine fumes going up his nose and the motion of the boat, saw to it that he was feeling very gravely butcher's hook.

And he looked it. His eyes were glazed and watery, his cheeks were flushed and red and his tongue was the colour of bad baby shit. His breath could have poached eggs.

Nope, Spewie hadn't brushed up at all well on that fateful day.

A split second after they'd moored up at the 12 Mile Reef, Spewie felt the first savage rush coming through his body. He headed for the side for the chunder of the century. If spewing was an Olympic event, he would have been the first athlete in history to win gold, silver and bronze in the one event. It was a chunder of classic proportions. A projectile vomit that hit the water a good 2 metres from the boat.

Chuck patted his dad's head: 'You'll be right, mate, just get it over and done with and let's do some fishing.'

His dad lifted his head to speak but was drawn back to the water by another incredible rush that started at his toenails. By the time it came out of his mouth his whole body was quivering from the impact.

After Spewie had roared like a wounded bear and heaved into the next postcode, he lifted his head to say something, only to be overcome once more with nausea.

'I know, Dad. You're trying to tell me you're OK,' Chuck purred.

'Fuckin' bullshit,' screamed his old man, determined to get the words out between heaves. 'I've just spat me fuckin' chops. I forgot to take the bastards out before I got crook. Now every fang in me fuckin' head's on the bottom of the ocean with the fuckin' shark shit.'

Chuck soothed his father and persuaded him to wash his mouth out with a nice, cold beer. After a couple, Spewie accepted the fact that his choppers were gone for good. After a couple more he even had a giggle about it. They decided to fish on.

And as if Neptune was offering a fair swap, the snapper come on the bite. They loaded the boat with whopper reddies – great big fish with huge bumps on their heads. It was their best day ever. They couldn't believe their luck.

It was just on dusk by the time they wearied of catching the huge fish and decided to leave them biting. Spewie steered while Chuck cleaned the catch.

'Dad,' Chuck yelled, 'look at this!' In the dark he produced a set of blood-soaked dentures from a snapper's stomach. More fossicking produced the other half. 'Christ, Dad, you wouldn't read about it,' Chuck chortled. 'This bastard swallowed your dentures, both of 'em, and we caught him. You wouldn't believe it!'

His father was amazed. 'Gimme those,' he growled suspiciously. 'Let me wash 'em before I put 'em back in.'

Spewie disappeared to the back of the boat. Chuck could hear the washing noises as his dad washed the slime and snapper gut off the dental plate with the contents of a can of beer.

Chuck couldn't control himself any longer. He burst out laughing.

'Dad,' he chuckled. 'I'm sorry, I couldn't help myself. I played a joke on you. They're my teeth. I hid 'em in the fish for a laugh. Can I have 'em back now?'

'Bit fuckin' late,' came the reply. 'I tried the bastards on a couple of times and when they didn't fit I threw 'em overboard!'

Mugged in Paradise

It was like driving down the darkest alley in New York, knowing that sooner or later something dreadful was going to happen ... but we were in a boat, and it was broad daylight.

Just as we rounded the corner – so to speak – to safety, there they were, a gang of hoodlums intent on demolishing everything we had hanging off the back of the boat – baits, lures and teasers. Then they were on us. Mayhem.

Every rod buckled and every reel groaned as we were mugged by those notoriously tough louts of Hamilton Island, the whopper sailfish.

Our crew, Peter Kidd, Peter Street, Aussie Tauranac and myself, were fishing the annual Hamilton Island Dunhill billfish bonanza aboard Aussie's superb 16 metre gamefishing boat *Capricorn*. It was our second day out.

On Day 1 we pulled the wrong rein and went south of Hamilton in search of the elusive sailfish. Nothing. The bite was up north of Hayman.

And weren't they biting! Every boat that fished that area had fish. Some had two, three, even four hooked up at once.

Next morning we were there at sparrowfart for a copybook start. We'd tagged and released a nice little sailfish of around 40 kilograms by

10 am. To make it even better, we had a film crew on board. They couldn't believe it.

That little sailfish had done everything right for the cameras. I had a combination of garfish baits, lures and a teaser trolling over the back, and he came up and had a good look at all of them. He moved from one to the other and drove us nuts for about 10 minutes as we tried to tease him into biting.

In the end he got really pissed off and I fed him a freshly rigged wolf herring bait, which he gutsed down. He jumped all over the ocean and performed beautifully at the side of the boat as we tagged him and sent him on his way. The cameraman was ecstatic – great footage, and early in the day.

By midday we were in the thick of it – but no more bites. In a 6 kilometre radius there were 16 game boats trolling baits and lures for sailfish. We had fish jumping all around us.

Sailfish were free-jumping all over the place, and as many as four boats at a time would hook up within our visual range. The place was crawling with fish. And still we couldn't get a bite.

We had a few lookers come up and inspect our trolled offerings, but they wouldn't go on with it. We were disappointed, to say the least. I rigged and re-rigged the baits and tried lures with brighter colours.

At three o'clock every boat around us was playing a fish. This was the hottest spot of the day. A concentration of sailfish that sent little packs out to maraud – or so it seemed.

And so we trolled through the mayhem. Something had to happen – and it did. We got mugged. I'm not sure how many there were, probably 10 of them, and all around 60 kilograms. Certainly formidable opponents on the 8 kilogram line we were using.

In a split second they were on us. Gangs of sailfish don't muck around. Each one knows that if it doesn't get in first, there's another waiting in line who will.

The first one came up and smashed the bright pink lure trolled in the wake. Before Peter had time to grab the rod, another pulverised the garfish bait and took off for New Zealand. In the instant that it took for

Sailfish are one of the most formidable opponents that swims ... that's if you can get one in the boat.

all this to happen, another three had demolished the two remaining lures. To add to the confusion, four more were attacking the huge hookless teaser we had hanging off the back – it was attached to 450 kilogram breaking strain sash cord.

I had never seen anything like it. We all had fish on at once, and they were jumping all over the ocean in different directions.

One line crossed another – instant bust-up. One gone. Another one threw the hook. Two down. The light wire on the double hook rigged garfish line gave out. Three gone.

There was just mine left – about 60 kilograms of hopping mad sailfish jumping around the boat. Just when it looked as if I was solidly hooked up, one of his mates picked up the teaser hanging in the wake of the boat and stretched the sash cord to breaking point, at exactly the moment my fish ran my line over it. Gone.

It was all over in a minute. They left us with smashed gear and smashed reputations. Even an old fisho like me had trouble coming to terms with what had just happened.

Our crew was in a state of shock. The camera crew were speechless. In 60 seconds that gang of thugs had wreaked havoc and bolted off into the blue.

Then we heard yelling and screaming coming from a boat a couple of hundred metres away. They had half a dozen fish on at once and within a minute they also had nothing left. The same gang, no doubt about it.

I'm glad that none of us was wearing anything valuable. The bastards would have jumped into the boat and mugged us for our wallets.

Pity the Poor Old Fishing Poms

If you are a person of generous nature, next time you're settled back with an ice-cold beer and catching a feed of fish, spare a thought for the poor old fishing Poms.

To them, a great day's fishing is a couple of carp. That's right ... carp. You know, those things that we Aussies despise. Those introduced pests that are wrecking our inland waterways and must be killed on sight by law. The Poms love 'em.

In the Old Dart it's a case of making do with what you've got, and a catch of carp is enough to gladden the heart of any angling Choom. Poor buggers. I wonder if they eat 'em. Yuk!

But while the dreaded carp is the jewel in England's inland angling crown, there are a few other species that are there for the catching in the rivers, canals and lakes. Things with depressing names such as bream (pronounced breem), tench, roach, chub, dace, minnows and bleak.

To add further insult to injury, collectively these species are known as 'coarse' fish; the salmonoids — trout and salmon — were always considered the fish of the gentry, because they were usually caught from a stream or a lake on some rich squire's property.

And according to the aristocrats and their hangers-on, the rest, the common species caught in the rivers and canals, were the species of the peasants — the 'coarse' populace, the ruffians who made up the general public. And the coarse folk of Britain accepted it without question, as they always did, for fear of having their heads cut off.

Yet despite all this, fishing in England is bigger than God's undies. And it's all because the enterprising Brits have a system of fishing called 'bank fishing', so named because they fish from the river bank.

But while we may snigger at the Poms as they sit on a river bank freezing their freckles off fishing for species that you and I consider pests, they have also turned this pastime into one of the biggest outdoor spectator sports in Europe. Fishing is 99% boredom and 1% frenzy – people all over the world acknowledge this – so to my mind, anyone who can turn fishing into a spectator sport is a genius. At least that's one up for the Poms.

Glued to the telly on one of those obscure stations on Fox, I've watched Pommie fishing shows which feature coarse bank fishing 'matches' – these competitions carry large cash prizes. Up to as many as 30 anglers are allocated side-by-side spaces known as 'pegs': each 'peg' consists of a few square metres of space from which the angler can fish into the river.

Champion Pommie angler Ian Heaps. He quit his job in a sheet metal factory to take up fishing full-time.

Anglers are allowed to use more than one rod at a time. Each fish they catch is placed into their individual keeper net in the water and every half hour or so the contents are weighed and recorded and returned to the water. The angler with the heaviest total weight at the end of the day wins.

The contestants are allowed to use any legal tackle and as much berley as they like; this usually comes in the shape of hand grenades which are thrown out to a spot of the angler's choice. He then casts his line into it.

At the major tournaments, spectators gather in their thousands on the opposite shore to cheer on their favourites.

136

The competitors who win consistently become sporting heroes and get to compete on the lucrative coarse fishing circuit all over Europe. This circuit includes such fishing hotspots as Ireland, Poland and Bulgaria. Some anglers even get to represent their country in the World Fishing Championships.

One such individual who competed and became World Champion was Cheshire angler Ian Heaps. I'm sure most English fishing enthusiasts will be familiar with him. After his win, Ian quit his job as a sheet-metal worker and became a full-time fishing competitor, lecturer and fishing tackle representative, and official Angling Advisor to the Northern Ireland Tourist Bureau.

Maggot-ace Dave Thomas with a handful of his plump wrigglers.

Ian even wrote a book about his success, called *Ian Heaps on Fishing*, in which he tells us about the adventures he has had on rivers around the globe (Australia doesn't get a guernsey) while defending his title and about the lifelong friendships he has formed with other anglers.

One such character is maggot-ace Dave Thomas, who specialises in breeding the plumpest wrigglers and impaling them on his hooks to enhance his hauls. I'd love to be a fly on the wall (no pun intended) at the dinner the night before an event as Dave puts a bit of work on a good sort. It would probably go something like this:

'Hi, baby. Like a drink?'
'No thanks. Sod off.'
'My name's Dave Thomas.'
'Not *the* Dave Thomas, the maggot-ace?'
'That's me.'
'Wow! I'll have a gin and tonic.'

Ian's book also includes chapters entitled *How To Be a Star* and *Life At The Top*. Boy, doesn't this bloke take himself seriously. He also mentions his catch of a 22.5 kilogram carp – at the time this was (and it probably still is) the English record.

Ian also offers hints about how to prepare for a match: be physically fit, don't get on the turps, and go to bed early the night before. He tells of the agony of having to choose between becoming a professional fishing person and travelling the world lecturing and fishing or staying with the lads at the sheet-metal factory.

He also provides fishing tips and hints for his doting public, and tells of his pride at being selected to represent his country – and then winning the World Championship at his first attempt. It's stuff that's not to be missed.

Sadly, the book is probably out of print by now, as it was published in 1982. You might find a copy around somewhere if you look hard enough. Sorry, I can't lend you mine. I need it for every time I get depressed. It cheers me up no end.

Ian netting his catch at a fishing competition in Bulgaria. Note the huge crowd on the opposite shore. As always, Ian was a real crowd pleaser with his one-handed netting antics.

The World's Luckiest Yank

Most people dream of catching a giant fish, but to this old fishing writer it's all too hard. I'd rather just go along for the ride, have a cold beer and photograph the action. But every so often I get conned into doing a bit of work ...

I don't catch many fish these days. I'm too old and lazy. My idea of a great day's fishing is hand-lining out of a boat for snapper over a cold tinny and shootin' the breeze with the boys. And if I don't catch a fish, who cares. It's the day that counts.

That's why I love my annual holiday out of Cairns with my old mate Captain Dennis 'Brazakka' Wallace, the world-famous Aussie gamefishing charter boat skipper. I ride along with him for 10 days or so each year and get pictures and stories of the giant black marlin his clients catch. And if I want to, I can do a bit of hand-lining for red emperor or coral trout.

Thanks to Brazakka, I've hobnobbed with a multi-billionaire from Arkansas, knights of the realm, legendary golfers, and the rich and famous from all over the world. Not bad for a kid who ran away to sea at 14 and could hardly read or write. Fishing has been very kind to me, which is fair enough, but that doesn't mean that I have to actually catch those giant fish any more.

Chamois Free

Leave me out of that back-breaking stuff where you sit in the game chair for hours on end. Been there, done that. These days I'm happy to let the paying customers do all that while I work up a sweat taking pictures and writing stories.

A few years ago Brazakka was fishing his boat for the season, the 14.5 metre *Kestelle*, at Opal Reef, about 80 kilometres northeast of Cairns. He had arranged a lift for me out to her on a Cairns-based 10 metre Bertram named *Chamois Free*, which was skippered by hotshot Miami captain John Phillips and crewed by deckie John 'Foxy' Fox.

'You'll have a good time with the boys,' Brazakka had told me. 'Just meet 'em on the wharf and load all your gear on, open a cold beer and they'll have you out here with me in a few hours, give or take catching a few marlin along the way.' It sounded all right to me.

The boys call their spasmodic trips out to the gamefishing fleet the 'mail run', and they troll baits and lures for giant marlin all the way, then deliver any letters, spare parts or urgent supplies to the crews on their arrival, stay on the boat overnight and fish all the way home the

following day. There isn't a mailman on Earth who wouldn't murder for a job like that.

After introducing myself to Captain JP and the Fox and as we pulled out from the Cairn's wharf with my bags safely in the cockpit of *Chamois Free*, I was introduced to Ken Newton, a veterinarian from Miami who was holidaying in Australia for the first time with his wife and baby son.

'So you're our angler for the day?' I inquired of the doc. 'It looks good out there – you might catch yourself a giant marlin.'

'No way,' he replied. 'I wouldn't know how to catch one of those things if my life depended on it. They told me this fishing photo-journalist was coming up from Sydney to do a story and that he was going to catch all the fish. I assume they mean you.'

I was trapped. The swines had got me nicely. Brazakka had obviously told them I was bone idle and that it was time I got a solid workout. I tried to escape, but it was too late. The boat was well on its way and there was no turning back. It was too far to swim and I couldn't insult my host. I had to just pray they didn't hook anything huge.

But who was this Yank? How did he fit into the act? 'Are you a friend of JP's from the States?' I asked.

'Never met him before in my life,' he replied.

I was intrigued. 'Are you a paying customer then?' I asked, knowing it was a stupid question, because if he was, why was I going to catch all the marlin?

'Quite the opposite,' he replied. 'These guys are paying me $50 to come out for a couple of days. This morning, when I was on my way to the tourist agency at the end of the wharf to make inquiries about taking my wife and baby son to see the koalas and kangaroos for the day, I stopped to look at his boat and he asked me if I'd like to ride out overnight because they had this mad journalist coming out and if they hooked into a monster marlin, they were a crewman short. My wife said it was too good an opportunity to miss, so here I am.'

I couldn't believe my ears. One minute this guy was walking down the wharf to get tickets for the family tourist trip, the next he was on his way out into the most prolific marlin waters in the world for a couple of days – and he was getting paid for it! Truth is stranger than fiction.

'JP's determined to get you a fish,' Foxy told me as he handed me earplugs to overcome the roar of the diesels.

'*Chamois Free* raises more marlin than any other boat in the fleet, and he'd love you to see how we do it so you can get some pictures and maybe do a story about us and the boat. He loves this old girl more than anything in the world. We're going to troll lures first and then I'm going to put out a special bait that I've been saving just for you. It's guaranteed to get us a giant marlin. Get a load of this.'

With that he went to the ice box and produced the biggest mullet I'd ever seen in my life. I went green as I looked at it. It must have been a metre long, and it was already rigged with a giant hook in its head and a wire trace – it was to be trolled behind the boat to catch a monster marlin.

Oh no! Not a mullet! I've spent the best part of a lifetime maligning mullet, and over the years I have written countless stories about how rotten they are to eat and how even my cats wouldn't eat one, even though they would eat their own young if given the chance. I've had a ball at the poor old mullet's expense. Every time I've been short of a story idea I've just dropped another bucketful on the mullet, and the readers have lapped it up.

And now here was a giant mullet sent to haunt me. Horror of horrors. The revenge of the giant mullet. I vowed there and then that I would never again say anything horrid about mullet. But was it too late? I was about to find out.

Fox put his prize bait back on ice. No sooner were the lures in the water than we hooked into a little black marlin of about 90 kilograms. I had it tagged and released in about five minutes.

Needless to say, the American vet was almost speechless with excitement as he watched that marlin jump all over the ocean, having never seen anything like it before in his life. I remember thinking at the time, what's this joker going to be like if we hook a whopper?

Then it was time to back off on the revs, put out the baits, do some leisurely cruising north and try to hook Mrs Huge (all giant marlin are

females). With a bit of luck we wouldn't, and I could sit back in the tropical sun and suck on a cold one.

But that particular dream of mine was not to be. The giant mullet bait was only in the water five minutes when a big black marlin cruised up to it and swallowed it the way my kid scoffs down a Big Mac. Whooshka! You'd think we'd hit it with a cattle prod – it was pounding across the surface and peeling line from the reel as if it were cotton from a bobbin.

I tried to convince JP that as I had already caught one fish, maybe our new chum, the vet, should take this strike. 'Are you serious?' JP yelled from the tuna tower.

Foxy the deckie holds up the giant mullet, rigged up as a bait. No one told the author that in fact it was a milk fish – which looks a lot like its southern cousin, the humble mullet.

'He's in no condition to talk, let alone fight a fish. Just get a load of him.' I looked at the Yank, who by this stage had his frothing tongue hanging loosely from the corner of his mouth; he was so delirious with excitement that all he could do was point at the fish and babble the words, 'Did you see that?' or something similar.

I somehow got the huge rod and reel out of the rod holder and staggered with it to the chair without being dragged over the side. Once harnessed in, I put my full weight on the fish and realised that I was going to be there for a while. After about 15 minutes my back felt broken, my arms were ready to drop off and my legs had turned to boiled spaghetti.

The Yank was rapidly approaching dementia – he was a candidate for the rubber room at the Betty Ford Clinic when, or if, he ever went home.

After an hour I'd had enough, but so had the fish, luckily. According to Foxy it was about 3 metres long and would have weighed about 250 kilograms. He took the trace and held the subdued marlin alongside the boat while I wobbled out of the chair and put a capture tag in it then cut it loose. The Yank leaned over the side, salivating and drooling at its size.

We cooled off with a beer, and an hour later the boys dropped me off at Brazakka's boat and tied up alongside for the night. The last I saw of the Yank, he was full of Bundy and Coke and falling about on the back of *Chamois Free* as the boys knocked him up an Aussie steak on the boat's barbie.

The following morning he was heard shrieking over a breakfast tinny, 'How long's this been going on?' as they headed back in the general direction of Cairns. We heard later on the two-way that JP and Foxy put the poor wretch onto a 500 kilogram marlin on the way home – mercifully, it jumped off after a titanic four-hour battle.

And me? I couldn't walk or move a muscle for a couple of days. Almost wrecked my holiday. I'll never say anything bad about a mullet again.

The world's laziest fishing writer in the fighting chair attached to a big fish and having to work hard for a change. It almost killed him.

Lureitis ... Fishing's Deadliest Disease

*There are many known fishing addictions and diseases —
but few known cures. Lying, boasting and cheating are
among the most common problems. But the most horrific
of them all is the piscatorial disease of the 1980s and
1990s, the totally addictive, outrageously expensive,
cruelly incurable and often life-threatening addiction
known throughout the fishing community as lureitis.*

Does someone close to you have this ghastly affliction? And would you know if they did? Read on and find out all about the piscatorial plague that threatens any angler who goes near a fishing tackle shop.

Browsing through a huge range of lures in a tackle shop the other day, I couldn't help but wonder just where it is all going to end. I mean just how many lures can they make? Just how many different shapes and sizes can the market absorb? After all, there are only so many lure fishermen out there. Or are there?

The market seems insatiable. I believe that it's due to the fact that most of the lures sold never see the light of day, let alone get wet, or, heaven forbid, get bitten by a fish. Crikey, we couldn't have that now, could we? Using one of those fantastic creations to actually try to catch a fish? No way.

I believe that there is a secret Lure Society out there. That's right. A clandestine gaggle of Australia's newest menace to society – lure gatherers – folk who are deeply and permanently preoccupied with a pastime that is almost as addictive as narcotics and that costs around about the same price for a fix.

Is your husband, mate, brother or son one of them? Do you suspect that the old man has got another woman or a shipment of dirty magazines? Does he sneak out at odd hours and lock himself in the garage or study? Does he talk to his mates in a dialect unknown to you that constantly refers to 'bibbed minnows', 'deep divers', 'fizzers', 'poppers' and 'mid-water runners'?

He does? Well, you poor wretch, you have my sympathy. He's got lureitis, and old Dr Kidd's here to tell you that it's incurable. If this highly addictive disease could get a guernsey in the dictionary I reckon it would read something like this:

> **lureitis** /ljur'it is/*noun* an incurable disease involving overwhelming infatuation with fishing lures, usually contracted by fisherfolk and fishing tackle shop staff; no known cure. Symptoms: red bulging eyes from staring at walls and walls of lures in fishing tackle shops and department stores, absence during the night for long periods at a time, usually spent fondling lures in garage or den. Treatment: take victim to as many fishing tackle shops as possible and let him gaze at the lures for long periods at a time; when he starts frothing at the mouth, blubbering and pointing, buy him the lure he is pointing at and lock him in a well-lit room with it until moaning subsides; beyond that it is hopeless; death usually occurs by drowning as the addict dives out of the boat to retrieve a beloved lure that is caught on a snag; addicts are also regularly taken by crocodiles when attempting impossible recovery techniques.

Yup, it's as bad as that. I've known blokes to let their families go without food and clothing while they spend the money on fish enticements. Normal blokes are doing time in the slammer for breaking into tackle shops in the dead of night to steal lures. Blokes who normally wouldn't get so much as a parking fine are doing time as habitual lure thieves.

It won't be long now before someone sets up Lures Anonymous to try to cure these poor wretches of this horrible addiction. There they will be, Halco lure catalogues in hand, telling everyone how they have to face the world one day at a time. And how they have to resist

The local tackle shop is where you'll usually find a lureitis victim, admiring the lures and drooling.

the urge to go to fishing tackle shops on the slightest impulse. And by listening to others, it may help. Yup, it's a strange old world out there.

My introduction to lureitis was back in the late 1960s, when I used to fish the rocks (a form of fishing called 'spinning') for gamefish such as yellowfin, striped and mackerel tuna, kingfish, tailor and salmon. I used highly polished chrome lures that looked like scurrying baitfish when they were retrieved rapidly.

I formed a fishing relationship with a certain Ronnie Rimmer, rock fisherman and legendary luremaker. Ronnie's main claim to fame was that he was the creator of the best lure I have ever used in my life for fishing the rocks.

Called the Rimmer Special, it was made of cast lead in a homemade mould. It was about 7.5 centimetres long, sliced at both ends, highly chromed, and looked for all the world like a whitebait shimmering just beneath the surface. And it was deadly on pelagics.

Although Ronnie used to sell his lures privately, I think for about a dollar each in those days, he always parted with them with a certain amount of reluctance – he was a bit like a breeder selling off a litter of pups. 'Now you make sure you look after them,' Ronnie would tell the purchaser as he fondled the lures before handing them over. 'Lot of work went into them. Treat 'em right and you'll get lots of fish.'

And true to his faith in his own product, Ronnie pounded the oceans daily from the rocks with his beloved Rimmer Specials, telling anyone who would listen that the shape of them was a special aerodynamic design that sent the fish off their rockers. Those lures were like Ronnie's kids, and he loved them with a passion. Yup, in hindsight, Ronnie had the worst case of lureitis I'd ever seen, but in those days I had no idea what it was. He used to talk about lures the way Bubba talked about shrimp in *Forrest Gump*. The poor bastard had it bad.

But then came the day when a lure broke poor Ronnie's heart. I have not seen or heard of him from that day to this. To him it must have seemed like a death in the family.

This lureitis victim has found paradise – his own lure manufacturing business.

This day we were spinning side by side at Ben Buckler, at the northern end of Bondi Beach, casting our lures up to 120 metres out to sea. Ronnie's lure had just hit the water, and as he clunked his old Mitchell 499 eggbeater into gear and took a turn of the handle, he found he was hooked up to a big fish.

It took off like a Bondi tram, testing the drag on Ronnie's reel to the limit. Just as it seemed the fish would empty his spool, Ronnie turned it, and the fight was on.

'Big yellowfin, I reckon,' he groaned as he lay back into his giant fishing rod, much to the awe of the Sunday crowd that had started to gather in the car park about 30 metres up on the cliff above us. 'Certainly bigger than anything I've ever had on before. Jeez, those little darlin' lures of mine just never let me down. Shame they can't cook and iron. I swear blind I'd marry one of 'em.'

The battle raged to and fro, to the urging of the crowd, which had now swelled to a couple of hundred cheering onlookers. At water level we couldn't see the fish, but the folk up in the car park could see how big it was as it fought hard on the surface.

'It's a bloody whopper, mate,' they yelled to Ronnie, who was by now loving every second of the attention. 'It's a bloody whale.'

And then it was at our feet, in the wash: it was a huge yellowfin tuna of around 40 kilograms. I readied the gaff. 'Just a couple more inches, Ronnie, and it's ours,' I yelled over the cheering of the crowd. 'Just walk back slowly and bring it closer to me and I'll gaff it.'

Ronnie gingerly stepped backwards, bringing the exhausted fish closer, inch by inch, to the gaff. I reached out, but just as I prepared the long rock gaff for the coup de grâce, something gave way and Ronnie fell over backwards ... I watched helplessly as the huge fish swam away.

'What the bloody hell!' Ronnie yelled. 'After all that, the bloody line broke.'

But I hadn't heard the familiar 'twang' of nylon busting. No, it wasn't the line. A horribly disappointed Ronnie wound in his line, and found – to his astonishment – that his beloved lure had broken in half.

I thought he was going to have a breakdown there and then. To him it was like finding out that his beloved wife had another bloke. He was a shot duck.

Ronnie was heartbroken. He didn't utter another word. He just picked up his gear and walked into the afternoon, never to be seen again. It was just about the saddest thing I've seen happen to a lure junkie.

But if there was ever a cure for lureitis, that would have to be it.

Women and Children First?
Not Always

I've been involved in a few life-threatening
circumstances over the years while fishing at sea, and no
matter the danger to those on board the boat, it was
always a case of women and children being rescued first,
even if it was at the cost of the lives of any of the men
involved in the situation.

After all, that is the unwritten law of the sea. But is that always the case? Apparently not – but more about that a little later.

Back in the early 1970s I was a deckhand on a fishing boat out of Port Stephens, on the NSW coast. We were heading back to port one afternoon when an unexpected squall from the south hit. The angry front was probably only about 3 kilometres wide, but its cracking lightning, blinding rain and gusting winds of up to about 60 knots whipped the sea into a frenzy and created waves up to 10 metres high. It was as black as hell and felt like the end of the world ... the Apocalypse ... Armageddon.

And then it was gone, leaving us to almost surf in on the giant waves it left in its wake. But others in smaller craft had been less fortunate. Between the headlands at the entrance to Port Stephens the shallow

water had created huge waves from the squall and lots of small fishing boats had been caught unawares.

Those who were wise to the ways of the sea in this neighbourhood had seen the disaster coming: they had cut their anchor ropes and fled rather than risk pulling the anchor up and being drowned or swept up onto the rocks.

As we steamed into the maelstrom we almost ran over a 6 metre cabin cruiser that was sinking before our eyes. The two men and one woman on board had put on lifejackets in readiness for their anticipated swim, but I doubt they would have survived if we hadn't come along.

The waves that were breaking over them and their boat were huge, and by the time we got to them almost all the boat had completely sunk. The bow was sticking about a metre out of the water, and they were clinging to it.

All the men could think about was the safety of the woman. 'Save Gladys, save Gladys,' they called as our skipper manoeuvred the boat close enough to throw a line and drag them aboard without swamping them in the horrendous seas. The men risked their lives by letting go of their boat and tying the rope around the lady – who, incredibly, seemed to be the calmest of them all.

Once she was secured to the lifeline we dragged her over to us, then over the tuck of our boat to safety. Around her neck she had her handbag, which was the only thing she had had time to grab before the boat sank. That's woman's intuition for you.

Then we brought the two blokes over the same way. I've never got over how concerned they were for Gladys, who turned out to be one of the men's wives. There was no hesitation in getting her to safety first, even if it meant them drowning.

One summer day on our way down to the Sir John Young Banks – off Nowra, on the NSW south coast – we came across a yacht that was sinking in dead calm seas after apparently striking a submerged object. Of the seven people on board, only the two children and the only woman were wearing lifejackets when we found them, clinging to their half-inflated dinghy alongside the stricken yacht, about a kilometre and a half offshore.

There had been no question that the three lifejackets they managed to grab as the yacht capsized should go to the kids and the woman. That's the law of the sea.

Special Constable John Whitehead, of the Sydney Water Police, tells me that they have never aided in a sea rescue where it has been anything but women and children first. That's the way it is in Australia – and, for that matter, most parts of the world. But not all.

The rule of 'women and children first' rather than 'every man for himself' seems to be as old as seafaring itself. The other really old unwritten law of the sea is that the captain always goes down with his ship, unless it is avoidable.

After a long voyage from England in 1878, the ill-fated passenger ship *Loch Ard* struck a reef off the Australian coast, and after seeing that all who could reach safety had, Captain George Gibb gallantly went down with his ship, in true British maritime tradition.

In 1852, when the troopship HMS *Birkenhead* struck a reef off South Africa, over 400 sailors and officers stood on deck and went down with their ship after the women and children had filled the only available lifeboats.

Whether or not a passenger liner's orchestra can be considered crew is debatable. Yet the *Titanic*'s band struck up a ragtime tune as the ship sank, and they sank with her. Hence the Harry Chapin classic song 'The Dance Band on The Titanic', which includes such classic lines as, 'The iceberg's on the starboard bow ... won't you dance with me?'

The *Titanic*'s pursers shook hands with First Officer Lightoller (he survived), and said, 'Goodbye, old man' and went down with their ship. The *Titanic*'s captain, Edward Smith, also went down with his ship – the last time Captain Smith was seen alive, he was saving a child.

Such acts of bravery are but a few in the long history of seafaring. But it doesn't always turn out that way. The sinking of the *Achilles Lauro* in 1994 brought with it tales of cowardice and looting by the Italian and South American crew members, and eyewitnesses reported them elbowing women and children out of the way to get to the lifeboats first.

Once there, there was no budging them. One officer even ripped off his uniform so that he would look like a passenger.

Passengers complained that the *Achilles Lauro*'s officers and crew showed little or no interest in the survival of passengers, and when survivors were transferred to a rescue ship from the lifeboats, some of the crew were already on board, showered and in fresh clothes. So much for gallantry.

The Greek liner *Lakonia* sank off Madeira in 1963, taking with it 125 British passengers – due to what the official inquiry described as 'gross negligence in carrying out procedures for abandoning ship' by the surviving captain and his crew.

But the classic of them all would have to be the captain of the *Oceanis*, which sunk off South Africa in 1991 without loss of life. The captain was the first over the side, with many of his crew in hot pursuit, much to the bewilderment of the 380 passengers. 'I couldn't care less what people say about me,' he later stated. 'When I say "abandon ship" that means everybody; it doesn't matter who gets off first, and that includes me. "Abandon" is for everyone.'

I wonder if he'd give his seat to a lady on a bus?

Mind-bending Marlin

The basic aim of sportfishing is for the angler to catch
as big a fish as possible on the lightest possible line
without breaking any of the rules. A fish weighing ten
times the breaking strain of the line used is brilliant,
15 to 1 is extraordinary and 20 to 1 is mind-boggling.
But there are some anglers out there who dare to go
even further than that.

A few years back I watched a bloke catch a 175 kilogram black marlin on an 8 kilogram breaking strain line and then let it go. Eight kilogram breaking strain line is what I use for catching 2 kilogram salmon and tailor off the rocks.

But when you consider that the same guy caught a 350 kilogram black marlin on a 6 kilogram line, the previous catch pales into insignificance. That's a weight-to-line ratio of 60:1, the equivalent of trying to hold an elephant on cotton! Impossible but true. I use 6 kilogram breaking strain line on 1 kilogram bream and flathead.

OK then, how could an angler land such a heavy fish on such light line? How could someone catch the most elusive gamefish of them all on a line that you and I use to catch flathead and bream? Skill? Luck? Being in the right place at the right time?

Sea Baby II

It's all of these things. And I'm going to tell you how they do it.

Regulation gamefishing and sportfishing has numerous breaking strain of line classes: 2 kilogram, 4 kilogram, 6 kilogram, 8 kilogram and so on, and the bigger the fish you catch on that line class the more likely it is to become a record in that section. There are strict rules that must be abided by, but there are ways in which those rules can be stretched.

I have always known how they catch huge sharks on light line for world and Australian record claims: they bend, but never break, the rules to the limit.

In most cases the poor old sharks, usually makos, whites or blues, are berleyed up to the back of the boat. Once the angler has determined that the fish could be big enough to be a new world record on a certain line class, he feeds it a bait attached to a regulation gamefishing outfit that fits the bill.

Because the International Gamefishing Association rule book states that the fish must be fought fairly, the anglers usually prod the poor thing with

The team (L to R): Bob Forbes with a hookless bait, Charles 'CP' Perry, Mike Levitt and Captain Paul Whelan on the bridge.

a boat hook so that it takes off from near the back of the boat, taking line with it as it goes. They then berley the shark back to the boat. This is called 'fighting the fish', and it manages to scrape through the anglers' loose interpretation of the rules.

Once it has been 'fought' back to the boat on denier-thin line, the crew whack a couple of flying gaffs in it and hang on for their lives.

The poor old shark doesn't know what hit it, and before long it's hanging up by its tail at a weigh station with the 'angler' standing alongside it telling everyone how clever he is and how he survived his brush with death.

What a crock of crap! So much for the great white hunters. These impostors make elephant poachers look like humanitarians.

Some of the shark records are bordering on the absurd. The late and great Bob Dyer was the first one to admit that his 484.44 kilogram white shark on 10 kilogram line is a classic example. Can you imagine *fighting* an 1100 pound shark to a grinding halt on a 20 pound line? Give me a break!

But the record books are riddled with them, and no doubt those records will still be standing long after they have laid me to rest.

While sharks are gullible enough to swim up to the back of a boat to be hand-fed, marlin and tuna are not so fearless, and they must be hooked in a different manner. And I doubt that anyone in the world would know more about catching huge fish on minuscule line than the famous American angler, Mike Levitt.

On my annual trip to Cairns several years ago, I was lucky enough to

spend a day on the Captain Paul Whelan-skippered *Sea Baby II* and watch Mike in action with his two hot deckies, Charles 'CP' Perry and local hotshot Bob Forbes.

As you're about to find out, the angler hasn't got a prayer without a good crew. Mike holds six world records with billfish (marlin and sailfish) caught on 1, 2, 4, 6 and 8 kilogram breaking strain line. He is the only man ever to catch an Atlantic sailfish and a black marlin on a 2 kilogram breaking strain line – this line is so flimsy that you or I could snap it with our bare hands.

So how does he do it? Simple. Outside the Great Barrier Reef off Far North Queensland, where the black marlin are as thick as the fleas on a cattle dog, the *Sea Baby II* trolls baits that have no hooks in them.

That's right ... no hooks. Crazy? Why would anyone spend all that money to come to Australia to charter the top light-tackle fishing act in the world and then troll baits without any hooks in them?

Because the baits are really 'teasers', and once a marlin rises to one of them and has a crack at it, it (the marlin) can't get hooked up. That's when the deckies drive the poor fish nuts by dragging the bait away and 'teasing' it into coming up to the back of the boat.

I saw one marlin get really pissed off. Every time it got the whole tuna bait in its cavernous mouth, one of the boys would drag the hookless bait away, leaving the marlin scratching its head and wondering what happened to lunch. The bamboozled marlin would then zero in on the other bait, and that too would be dragged away. The deckies kept it up and nearly drove the poor marlin nuts; eventually they 'teased'

Mike hooked onto a whopper on ultra-thin line.

it so close to the back of the boat that they could have reached over and patted it.

By now Mike had had a good look at the fish and decided what line class he would feed it. In this case the fish was about 175 kilograms, and he decided to catch it on 8 kilogram line. So when the fish was going gangbusters at the back of the boat, darting this way and that in sheer frustration, and ready to eat anything put in front of it, Mike presented it with a bait that had a hook in it. The marlin wolfed it down.

Having caught its prey, the marlin then swam off, going about its business – with the *Sea Baby II* in hot pursuit. As he was playing the marlin Mike explained to me that as long as the fish stayed on top, they would have a chance of catching it. If it took off into the bottomless abyss off the Continental Shelf, they had no hope on such light tackle.

But stay on top it did. It jumped many times, and each time it did, the crew breathed a sigh of relief that it didn't land on the spider's web-thin line. After an hour it was sitting on the surface about 100 metres away and Captain Whelan decided to have a crack at getting it.

He gunned *Sea Baby II* backwards and Mike wound line as fast as his arms let him. They were on top of the fish before it had a chance to know what was going on. CP had the trace in his hand; he took a couple of wraps and hung on while Bob stuck a numbered tag in the bewildered marlin – this would both prove the catch and aid researchers should it be recaptured elsewhere later. Then they cut the thick nylon trace and let it go.

They could have killed the fish and boasted of their conquest, but they chose to let it go. Imagine that – letting a 175 kilogram fish on 8 kilogram line go. In anyone's book it would be the catch of a lifetime. But not these guys. To them the super-abnormal is all in a day's fishing.

And they reckon it's easy when you know how.

The Dreaded Mal de Mer

*Have you ever been seasick? I have, just once, but it was
enough to let me know that it is about the worst
experience a human being can live through. And I had it
bad. It taught me the most important lesson I will ever
learn: fishing and booze just don't go together.*

The night before that monumental heave, I'd been on the sherbet
something terrible at a mate's wedding, and I was still half tanked
when I rolled up at the boat at 6 am. Even though the sea was as
flat as a billiard table, the rushes came upon me as soon as we cleared
Sydney Heads, and by 8 am I was bringing up the lining of my stomach.
By midday any negative thoughts I had ever about euthanasia had flown
out the window. By mid-afternoon I was begging the skipper to radio for a
helicopter, to hell with the expense, to mercy-dash me out of there.

But some good always comes out of bad. At least that day I found out
who my mates were. None of the guys on the boat, that's for sure. We
had only chartered the boat for a bit of bottom bouncing in the
morning, but as the fishing was so good, my so-called best buddies paid
the captain a little extra to stay out all day.

And as they were such a sympathetic lot, they fried up hamburgers with
bacon and runny eggs for lunch and ate them in front of me with the yolk
running down their chins, then washed the lot down with cans of VB.

I was so sick I thought I'd have to go to hospital. As it was I spent a couple of days at home in bed getting over it. Touch wood, I've never been crook since, and there's no way I'd run the risk of it happening again by getting on the turps the night before a fishing trip. I learned my lesson the hard way. Fortunately, I'm one of the lucky ones who doesn't suffer from the dreaded mal de mer.

But I feel awfully sorry for those who do. And there are plenty of the poor buggers out there. You won't see many of the habitual sufferers on the water, though, because eventually it stops them going anywhere near boats or the briny. I've known folk to have it so bad that they get crook skindiving or surfing. And I've known others who have persisted week in and week out for years and never beaten it.

On the other hand, I've known a handful of dedicated anglers who have beaten it through sheer determination. Before he died at age 80, a few years back, fishing legend Jack Farrell, of Sydney's Watsons Bay, had been to sea with the likes of Zane Grey, Bob Dyer and Jack Davey for nigh on 70 years. But until the day he collapsed with the brain tumour that ultimately killed him, Jack still got crook at sea.

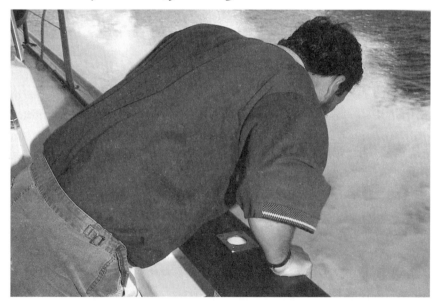

This poor devil's got the anti-seasickness ear patch on – but even that didn't work.

I fished with him a hundred times and he just accepted his 'complaint' the way asthma and hay fever sufferers accept theirs. But to make life at sea as bearable as possible, Jack had a set of rules he swore by. Those rules, along with a few suggestions of my own, may make your day out a little more pleasant. Here goes:

- Never drink lots of alcohol the night before a fishing day. It's a definite no-no!
- Have a substantial breakfast but make sure you avoid dairy and animal products. Bacon, eggs, sausages and milk are strictly out. Fruit, dry toast with Vegemite or baked beans, black coffee or tea and vegetable sticks (such as celery and carrots) are great stomach fodder; if you're going to be ill, it's a good idea to have something solid in your stomach. Besides, the thought of any of that other greasy gunk inside you is enough to make you want to throw up anyway.
- The best drink on a boat is Coca Cola – the original Coke, not Diet. And if you can get it in those small bottles with the bottle-opener tops, not the screw tops, it works 100% better. Don't ask me why, it just does. It helps you belch and get rid of the pressure on your stomach. The next best thing is any sort of fizzy drink, perhaps lemonade or soda. Anyone who drinks grog all day on a boat is a moron. Drunks are a pain in the butt at the best of times, but on a boat there is no escaping them and they usually wind up crook. A cold beer out of the Esky on the way home is the perfect way to end the day – but it's not acceptable before then.
- Stay out in the fresh air and avoid going into the cabin or saloon. If the boat has a flying bridge, that's the ideal place to be. If it hasn't, get up near the bow and get some fresh air through your lungs. And whatever you do, stay away from the engines and the fumes. There is nothing more likely to send a potential chunderer off than some nice toxic diesel or petrol fumes up the Lionel Rose and into your lungs. Yuk, I can almost taste 'em now, and it's making me crook just sitting here at my desk. So it's not hard to imagine what they'll do to someone who's already halfway there.

- Don't read. Forget about getting into the latest Tim Winton novel or the Sunday papers. This is a sure-fire way to get butcher's hook. I don't suffer from seasickness, but after reading for about 10 minutes in the cabin even I'm ready to have an up-and-under over the side. I'm not a gambling man, but I'll bet a nugget to a nannygai that even old King Neptune himself would get crook if he read a book in the cabin, downwind of the engine fumes.

- Try the anti-histamine seasickness tablets, but don't take too many — if you do, you'll crash all day, and if you're going to do that, there's no point going fishing. The 'patches' seem to be very effective; they drip-feed the anti-histamine into your system, which keeps drowsiness to a minimum.

- Show a little sympathy for the victim and try to get him/her involved in the fishing or in looking at the landmarks. Do anything you can to get the person's mind off their predicament. Tormenting victims, particularly women, is a low act and damns the prey to a day of indescribable misery. Be fair.

Now that you know all the known cures, or should I say 'suggested preventives', let's look at the cause of the dreaded mal de mer.

My friend Dr Julian Pepperell, the Professor Julius Sumner Miller of marine biologists, tells me that seasickness is caused by the constant motion of the boat. This creates an imbalance in the middle ear — the middle ear is a series of tiny semicircular canals that criss-cross each other and act as sort of spirit level to keep us balanced; it lets the brain know when we are the right way up and the wrong way up.

When we are rocked around a lot, the brain gets the wrong signals from the middle ear and loses co-ordination. With some people the body reacts by getting confused, which results in mild to extreme nausea. The motion sickness pills dampen nerve impulses the same way aspirin does for a headache.

Going out on a boat all day and being sick is like giving someone a $100 note and a baseball bat and telling them to bash you. Unless you

are the world's most dedicated angler or yachtie, you'd never do it on purpose. Or would you?

60 Minutes reporter Charles Wooley gets seasick in rough conditions, yet a few years ago he took part in a Sydney to Hobart yacht race in order to get a story for the program. Although proud of the fact that he survived until a mammoth storm hit during the second day, Charlie spent the next two days below decks with a bucket and fewer comforts than a man on death row. That's dedication for you.

But I know plenty of blokes who wouldn't set foot on a boat for a million dollars a minute. And after having been there and done that, albeit only once, if I got crook every time I went out, I don't blame 'em one little bit.

My Mate of the Sea

*My mate of the sea is the grey nurse shark. I'm a
Taurean (11 May), and the grey nurse's proper name is*
Carcharias tauras. *To my mind that makes us mates.
But thanks to us red-blooded Aussies, my mates are in
grave danger of becoming extinct in eastern Australian
waters in the next 20 years or so.*

According to a recent survey conducted by dive shop operators along the lower east coast of Australia, there are only a few hundred grey nurse sharks in existence between Flat Rock in southern Queensland and Montague Island in the south.

Where there were once thousands of these harmless, docile cave dwellers that grow to about 4 metres and 300 kilograms, there are now just a few. The rest have either been speared, caught on rod and reel or blasted to death with power-heads — these lethal spears have a shotgun cartridge in the tip that explodes on impact.

Even the fact that they were put on the endangered species list in the early 1980s — which means that anyone who is caught in possession of one is subject to a huge fine and/or jail — hasn't stopped their sad decline. Despite the ban, an average of three people have been caught killing them each year.

Scuba divers have found many that have been captured and returned to the water alive to die an agonising death with their fins hacked off. Nurses swimming about with shark hooks and wire traces hanging from their mouths are commonplace.

Combine this with these facts – a mother only produces two pups every two years, there are lots more boy nurses than there are girls, and they are cannibals by nature – and things aren't looking good for my mates of the ocean.

In fact, things have never looked crash hot for the poor old grey nurse. For as long as I can remember, the nurse was an animal of dread, a deadly man-eater that must be avoided at all costs and killed on sight.

How it got that reputation is anyone's guess, because nothing could be further from the truth. I believe it was the name. Whaler, tiger, white pointer, hammerhead, mako … all the other sharks sound so boring. But *grey nurse*. Now that was a name that could be sensationalised. And it was.

Through the 1960s and 1970s, before we knew that sharks were beautiful creatures and that grey nurses weren't deadly man-eaters at all

The grey nurse's fangs are in fact ripping, not biting teeth, and are not designed to bite humans in half.

but old slugs with teeth that couldn't de-flea a cattle dog, let alone bite a human in half, they were the most hated beast on the planet.

Throughout the 1970s a bloke named Alf Vockler (we called him Ralph Shockler) rang up the Sydney radio stations at least once a week and told them that there were huge schools of man-eating grey nurse sharks surfing down the face of waves in Sydney Harbour and that anyone who swam in there was in danger of being eaten alive.

We often wondered if the fact that Alf owned the swimming baths at Watsons Bay (he also always gave a plug for them) had anything to do with these reports – was he trying to scare a few clients out of the harbour and into his pool?

And you must have also seen the ancient footage on Cinesound News of Ben Cropp or Ron and Valerie Taylor bravely swimming down to a poor old grey nurse and giving it what-ho with a shotgun power-head to the voice-over of 'and there goes another savage man-eater that won't be taking any Australian bathers in the surf this year'.

We big brave gamefishermen weren't much better. We used to catch nurses – if you could call it 'catching'; it was more like just winding the handle on the reel – and hang them up on the gantry at the Sydney Game Fishing Club for the public to ogle. Then they would all say how brave were to rid the sea of such hateful critters.

So now, thanks to us being boneheads over the years, there are only a few left. But the scuba divers who make a living by taking folk for dives with these docile denizens have a scheme that, while it may not be to everyone's liking, may work to get the stocks back to a point where they are not under threat.

Grey nurses certainly look the part, but they are harmless cave dwellers.

'There are 13 spots along the NSW coast which are grey nurses' habitat,' says South West Rocks Dive Centre honcho Noel Hitchins, 'and we reckon that if we can get 500 metres around each of these areas declared a marine sanctuary, the grey nurses have got a chance.

'That would mean no fishing or spearfishing at all within that zone, just scuba diving. That way we could be sure that no one would be catching them or leaving them with wire traces and giant fish hooks, which could only be intended to catch sharks with, hanging out of their mouths.

'We conducted a survey along the coast in conjunction with NSW Fisheries, and it resulted in only 297 grey nurses being sighted,' Noel says. 'But in a recent NSW Fisheries overview, based on our survey, they only recommended that restrictions be placed upon boats fishing in the areas – not a total ban.

'Regulations are now that in the 13 sites along the NSW coastline that are recognised as "critical habitat" for the grey nurse shark, boat anglers are not allowed to *anchor up* and fish with baits. They can still troll lures through the areas – this doesn't affect the grey nurses, as they don't rise to the surface to take lures, but it doesn't stop fishermen from berleying and drifting through the areas with big baits, which still gives them every opportunity to catch and harm a grey nurse.

'But there are no restrictions on wire traces, or on commercial vessels set-line fishing. We're not happy with that. We know more about the movements and breeding of these sharks than anyone, and if we can't get a total "no take" fishing ban in the areas, we want to at least come pretty close.'

I'll drink to that. Save my mates, I say. As a fisherman, I don't generally believe that one recreational activity should have exclusive use of a natural resource; I think fishos and divers should have an equal opportunity. But in this case I'm prepared to accept that maybe these areas should have stricter restrictions. I'd even agree with no fishing whatever.

Let's hope that sometime in the future that the powers that be wake up to the fact that the future of the beautiful, harmless grey nurse is worth the sacrifice of having to find another spot to fish.

Things That Sting

Fish have been known to even up with anglers, and there
are more than a few that are capable of giving you a
fishing trip you won't forget in a hurry. Top of the list is
the old stonefish. He not only didn't answer roll-call
when looks were being handed out – he also got more
than his share of venom, and is spoken of with horror in
tropical Australia.

'Bloody horrible things, those stonefish,' my dad told me when
I was a kid. He insisted I wear thick-soled shoes when
wandering around the reefs of Perth at low tide. He said that
if I trod on one I would die a horrible death within seconds and he
couldn't afford to bury me.

Stonefish possess 13 dorsal spikes with poison glands and are capable of
injecting extremely painful venom into a human foot. With this in mind,
my mates and I set about murdering any fish that remotely resembled a
stonefish, convinced that we were ridding the West Australian coastline
of a menace far worse than the communists, which were all the rage in
the 1950s.

What Dad didn't tell me was that while the stonefish was a carrier of
deadly toxin, it hadn't actually killed anyone in Australia yet; not even

those few who had trodden on them in remote reef areas on the Great Barrier Reef in faraway northern Australia.

And while Dad had put the fear of God into me about stonefish, I was already aware of another charming WA resident called the 'blowie' or 'puffer-fish'. This little charmer had no external pain-inflictors, but if you ate one you died immediately, in excruciating pain. I would find out years later that in the eastern states the same fish was called a toadfish.

Yep, the old blowie was knockin' 'em down like flies when I was a kid. The victims were always Asians, of whom we didn't see many after the war. The rumour was that they liked any sort of fish at all, and to them the blowie looked just like a delicacy back home, wherever that was. So when they caught a bunch of blowies, they thought they'd won lotto. They went home and cooked 'em up, and they all died in agony that very night. And it happened lots of times. Or so my dad said.

I can only ever recall seeing one report in the paper about anyone dying of blowie poisoning, so while I knew that they contained a deadly toxin, I still wasn't too sure whether or not Dad had his facts straight. Maybe he heard those stories from the same folk who told him about the stonefish deaths and the communists.

One of the most innocent yet prickliest customers around is the humble bream, but the amount if pain it can inflict varies according to where you catch it. The bream's prickles don't carry any venom as such, but if you catch them in a nasty environment, then the bacteria carried on their spikes can enter your bloodstream through the prick and cause you no end of misery.

Many years ago in Sydney I used to fish the rocks near a sewage treatment works, and on more than one occasion I had my hand flare up in a nasty poisoned bulb after it had been impaled on a bream spike. As he filled me up with antibiotics, the doctor explained that it was the muck from the effluent that caused the agonising swelling, not the spike from the bream – it was not guilty on all charges.

The same thing goes for the flathead, redfin and the barramundi, all of which are capable of inflicting nasty wounds from their spikes – these

The poor old stonefish would never win a beauty contest, but he more than makes up for his looks by having a venomous sting that is capable of killing a human.

seem to have been designed by Mother Nature for no other reason than to cause as much pain as possible to humans.

It is worth noting that the larger the flathead gets, the bigger the spike on the gill cover plate; it's a good idea to keep away from that area when handling a 'lizard', irrespective of its size. I can assure you that having a large flathead's entire spike go into your body is not a pleasant experience. It's something that the body's system doesn't take too kindly to, either – it reacts with considerable pain.

Another dangerous area is the edge of a barramundi's gill cage. It is as sharp as a razor, and many a nasty cut has been inflicted on unwary anglers as they pick them up to release them.

The humble leatherjacket can be an unpleasant customer as well. While that dastardly looking spike on its back may not eject any poison when it stabs you, the rough area just below the spike is a natural collector of nasties, and if the spike is embedded in your skin, the unfriendly bacteria stay in the wound and cause awful pain. Leatherjackets should be handled with the utmost care at all times.

Parrotfish have a beak just like a parrot, so putting your hand too close to one of them is not recommended. And the old octopus has a beak like a Major Mitchell cockatoo, and has been known to inflict nasty bites on the unwary.

Stingrays won't bite you, but that rough tail is their built-in defence mechanism, and many a chafed and raw leg has been the result of a run-in with the normally passive stingray. My suggestion is to stay away and let them go about their business. If you catch one on a line, just cut it free and avoid what could be an unpleasant confrontation.

A few years back on Lizard Island, about 200 kilometres north of Cairns, I was fishing off the back of the boat and caught a fish that the locals call a 'happy moment'. How wrong could they be. Before they could tell me not to grab hold of it to get the hook out, I had wrapped my hand around it and it had stung me on the hand with about a dozen of its spikes.

Ouch! Happy moments indeed. I was in agony. The locals suggested that I urinate on my spiked hand to cure it. They laughed their heads off as muggins me went right ahead. It didn't cure the pain.

Just like the guy who was bitten on the bum by a snake and his mate radioed the Flying Doctor, who told him he had to suck the poison out or his mate would die within minutes.

When his mate asked him what the Flying Doctor said, he replied, 'He said that you are going to be dead in a couple of minutes.'

The Sharks of Sugartown

*This is Sugartown folklore – and, I was told,
a true story. It was told to me by the locals when I
was forced to stay there overnight when my friend's
Porsche blew a radiator hose. Sugartown doesn't
have a Porsche dealership.*

On the Pacific Highway between Ballina and Grafton, on the
north coast of New South Wales, is the tiny township of
Broadwater. The local industry is sugar, so the township is
known as 'Sugartown'.

Consisting of a pub, service station and the usual small collection of
country shops, the highlight of Sugartown is the NRMA depot, which is
on the other side of the highway from the pub. From their regular possies
at the bar, the locals watch the daily procession of vehicles and occupants
towed into the depot. Most of these poor wretches have broken down
along the highway; a call for help from their mobile phone has them
under tow to the comfort of the depot in no time at all. The measure of
their dilemma is then assessed, and the appropriate action taken.

In most cases the vehicles can be repaired on the spot, but when
special parts are needed, a stay in the rooms at the back of the Exchange
Hotel until the bits are flown up from Sydney – which usually takes a
day and a night – is arranged.

Such was the case of the American tourist, Chuck, in his rented Cadillac. The poor bastard had blown a fan belt about 20 kilometres out of town and was rescued by none other than 'Knowledge', the local know-all and urger who just happened to be passing by in his shitbox ute.

On the drive into town they became great mates. Chuck was overwhelmed by his rescuer's assistance. Back at the NRMA depot, Knowledge arranged for the Caddie to be towed to town. When it was discovered that the car had blown an alternator and the parts wouldn't arrive until the day after tomorrow, he arranged accommodation for Chuck – and an introduction to everyone who was anyone in the bar – at the pub.

Knowledge had told Chuck that it was just 'good old Aussie hospitality'. Of course the tourist had no way of knowing that somewhere along the line it was going to have a dramatic effect on his wallet … Knowledge hadn't figured out the angle yet, but it was only a matter of time.

The following morning Chuck expressed his enthusiasm for fishing to his new best friend.

'Say, buddy,' he said, pointing to the Richmond River in the background. 'Do you guys ever catch any fish in that creek?'

'That creek, as you call it,' laughed Knowledge, 'just happens to produce the best shark fishing in the district – probably in Australia, for that matter.'

'You're bullshittin' me!' said the Yank in amazement. 'Surely no self-respecting shark would live there. It looks like it's runnin' upside down!'

Now Knowledge made it up as he went. There was a quid to be made here somewhere.

'No, not there,' Knowledge said, 'much further down river, towards the sea. A mate of mine's got a private island there that's only accessible by boat. He catches white pointers, tigers, makos – you name it, the joints crawling with 'em. They gather there in their thousands to feed on the run of giant sea mullet that gather at the mouth of the river to spawn.

'Trouble is, the spot's very exclusive and no one knows about it,' he continued. 'There's even a secret path through the cane fields to get to the beach to row out there. Just don't fall in on the way out. I can get you out there if you really want to go for the day. But it'll cost you.'

'How much?' Chuck asked.

'Mates' rates are a hundred bucks a day – that's the use of the boat and the whole island. Reckon I can get him down to eighty for you, seein' as you're a tourist and all.'

'That's a deal, mate,' Chuck said and shook on it. 'I'll get my gear out of the Caddie and we'll start right away.'

The 'gear' turned out to be a beach rod and one of those Japanese spinning reels. The Yank had bought it for catching whiting at Port Stephens, on the way north from Sydney.

'Not worth a crumpet,' said Knowledge. 'They'll smash that kid's stuff to shit. What you need is some heavy shark gear, about 50 kilo line, a Penn reel and a good stout rod. Mate of mine's got just the outfit, rents it out to guys lucky enough to get out to the island.' Knowledge fixed the Yank with another bleary stare. 'But it'll cost you.'

'How much?' he said.

'Going rate's about $50 a day but I'll get him down to forty for you, seeing as you're a tourist and all.'

'OK, let's go,' said Chuck.

'Hold it,' said Knowledge. 'What about traces and hooks? You're going to look pretty stupid out there with elephant gun gear and yellowtail hooks. I'll slip down to the hardware store and get it while you get changed. Twenty bucks should do it. You'll need bait – say half a dozen mullet. They're very expensive around here, so they'll cost you.'

'How much?' the Yank asked.

'Let's say another $10.' The Yank handed Knowledge the money.

'Tell you what I'll do,' Knowledge said. 'You being a tourist and all, I'll even run you up there and back – and the petrol's on me.'

It took Knowledge about ten minutes to 'borrow' 'Bluey' Howard's shark rod, reel and traces from his open garage. He wouldn't miss the gear for a day – he only used it when he went gamefishing down the coast.

Another ten minutes and he'd knocked off six poddy mullet from 'Stench' McKenzie's mullet trap and was back at the motel, ready to go.

Zane Grey was waiting, resplendent in sandals, long black socks, knee-length shorts, yellow and lime-green open-necked shirt, sunglasses, Panama hat and a cigar that looked like a dog turd.

'You're real friendly to tourists,' he said as they sped toward the 'secret spot' about 2 kilometres out of town.

The 'secret path' was about 10 metres wide and led straight through the Turner brothers' cane fields. In fact it wasn't a path at all; it was just a divider between areas of cane, and led down to a sandy little beach where the brothers kept their small dinghy, for when they occasionally fished the estuary for bream.

Without the divider, access to the beach was impossible, as the sugarcane grew right to the water's edge. The brothers didn't mind if anyone used it to get to the beach as long as they asked permission first. Knowledge was not the type to bother with such details.

'Watch out for the snakes,' he warned his new chum. 'The joint's crawlin' with 'em, all sorts of the bastards – death adders, copperheads, black snakes – and all as mean as buggery.'

The Yank fled the length of the open space in double-quick time. Knowledge tried to keep up with him but found it hard because he was pissing himself laughing. He knew full well that the snakes stayed in the cane unless something drove them out.

The exclusive island was about 100 metres away across the river. Knowledge showed him how to use the oars, loaded his gear and pushed him off.

'See you back here at five,' he yelled. The Yank waved as Knowledge headed towards the pub for an ice-cold ale and to hold court. He counted his money on the way – $150, not bad for a morning's work. Wait till the fellas hear this one!

By 2 pm, Knowledge was well and truly flyblown. Fate had been kind. He decided to wander into the TAB and have a punt. There was an immediate omen. 'Give me fifty on Yankee Joker in the third,' he yelled, throwing his money down.

Of course Yankee Joker bolted in at 20:1. Knowledge couldn't believe his luck – what a day! More drinks all round back at the Exchange and it was time to go. Lugging a carton of cans, Knowledge headed back to the beach to wait for his unwitting benefactor. As drunk as he was, he could still make out the boat on the island. He couldn't see the Yank, though. Knowledge tried to ponder the significance of this but passed out in the warm sand.

It hadn't taken Chuck long to figure out that there was something peculiar about shark fishing prospects on the island. The water around the island for about 20 metres out was very shallow and sandy. Maybe they were long, flat sharks. Needless to say, after hours of patient angling his cunningly rigged mullet was still untouched.

The Yank decided to take a walk around to the other side of the island. A few minutes later he parted some bushes to find, to his absolute astonishment, a bridge linking the island to the mainland. And there were several people on the bridge, pulling in bream, flathead and whiting galore – he had tumbled onto the local hotspot.

Still not aware that he had been got, he inquired of an angler, 'Caught any sharks?'

'Are you crazy, mister?' the angler said. 'The last shark seen around here was when the local car dealer fell in!' Many thoughts crossed the Yank's mind as he walked back towards the boat and shark alley.

The first sign of trouble was when Knowledge felt hot ashes falling all over him. He ignored them at first, brushing the cinders from his hair and face and nuzzling back into the beer carton, which was now his makeshift pillow. He felt more hot ashes, then the roaring and heat of – 'Shit, no!' – a cane field fire.

Oh no! The Turner brothers had chosen today to put the fire through their cane fields, as they did every season. Now it was heading towards the river, the way it always did. Knowledge woke to a towering wall of smoke and fire heading in his direction.

But that was the least of his worries. He nearly died of shock when he saw what was wriggling out of it. Snakes! Hundreds of 'em. And all heading for his little beach. There were two alternatives: be bitten or drown. Somehow Knowledge had never had the time to learn to swim. Neither prospect appealed.

Then a third possibility presented itself. Sitting out in the middle of the channel was the Yank, in his little boat. He seemed totally in awe of the spectacle. It looked as if hell had opened up, yet in a few short minutes it would be all over; the fire would reach the river bank, the end of its journey – and most certainly the end of Knowledge.

Knowledge hit a snake with a beer can. 'Give us a hand, will ya, mate?' he yelled to Chuck.

'Why, are you scared of the sharks?'

The beach was now a wriggling mass of serpents.

'Ah, come on, mate,' Knowledge said.

'All right', said the Yank, 'But it'll cost you.'

'How much?'

'How much have you got?' asked the Yank.

'I got a grand,' said Knowledge, knee deep in death adders.

'Well the going rate for a rescue of this sort is a couple of grand, but seeing as you are a local and all ...' the Yank said as he picked up the oars.

Things That Float

*You never know what you'll find floating around
out there in the middle of the ocean, and running
into solid objects in a boat causes more disaster than
most other boating hazards combined. But apart
from being a danger, floating objects are also fish
havens, so it's always worth a look to see what's
living underneath them.*

Every time I read that a boat has gone missing at sea without a trace, I automatically wonder what it hit. There are so many floating objects out there that going to sea these days is like tap dancing through a minefield.

I've seen humpback, pilot and southern right whales, countless sunfish, shipping containers, huge tree trunks, dead dogs, sheep and cattle, and even an old Silent Knight refrigerator floating around in the ocean.

Every one of them is capable of sinking your boat and killing you if you hit it.

Any ocean-going fisho will tell you that floating debris (the bigger the better) is a godsend – in terms of fishing – because huge concentrations of fish, usually mahi-mahi and kingfish, congregate under it and are easy to catch. But more of that later.

However, floating objects are much more treacherous than they are useful as fish attractors.

Even boats decked out with the latest in safety equipment have disappeared off the face of the Earth without so much as a bleep from an EPIRB or a Mayday over the radio. When you consider that it takes only seconds to activate the radio beacon or get on the two-way, those boats must have gone down pretty darn quickly.

There's no doubt that the most treacherous things that float are the huge containers which fall off the container ships; they are designed to float just a few feet beneath the surface so that they can be recovered if they're found. If you hit one, it's Goodnight Dick, because they open up the front of the boat like a can of sardines and it sinks head first in an instant.

I imagine it happens so quickly that you're drowning before you know what's happened. No doubt there are people in the world who've hit containers and survived, but I've yet to meet one.

I heard a whisper once that there were moves afoot to produce a device that would sink containers after they'd been in the water for a specified time. Something like a dissolvable bung which would eventually let water in so it could sink to the bottom.

A fantastic idea, but would the container companies and their insurers outlay an arm and a leg to sink a fortune's worth of whatever and lose all hope that one day it might be recovered and returned by another ship?

Besides, the odds that a vessel would run into one are of the needle-in-the-haystack size – you would have more chance of being trampled by a wildebeest while flying on the Concorde from Fiji to Tasmania with Frank Sinatra piloting and Madonna pouring the drinks with no gear on.

Most boats that come to grief in the shipping lanes of the world are either commercial fishermen or long-distance yachties. We recreational anglers rarely venture out that far, but we still have a lot to contend with in the way of floating debris, particularly after torrential rain, when the creeks and rivers flush out the estuaries. Anything from dead animals to bales of hay are swept out to sea.

I'd also like a dollar for every time we've sucked a plastic garbage bag up into the engine cooling intake of the boat or got one caught around the propeller on the outboard. But that's one of the facts of boating life today. I doubt that people will ever learn that plastic bags are the worst possible thing you can throw overboard – they are probably responsible for more boating mishaps than any of the other 10 items combined.

The beautiful old sunfish has a lot to answer for as well. I'd hate to think how many boaties I know who have bent a prop or damaged their hull by running over a sunfish as it lolled around on the surface with its giant fin flopping from side to side.

The huge, moon-shaped sunfish grow up to a tonne and can be as deadly as a floating mine if you hit them. That aside, they're the most lovable creature that swims, neither carnivore nor predator, preferring to graze on bluebottles, jellyfish and plankton.

To my mind, a lot of the boats that disappear without trace within sight of land have probably been going too fast and hit a sunfish. Although they can do plenty of damage and most definitely can cause death, I know of a dozen boats that have hit them and lived to tell the tale.

Floating logs are another deathtrap, and while I've only ever seen a couple of floating containers, I've seen more than my fair share of logs.

Some of the commercial logs I've seen defy imagination – I can only assume that they must have fallen off log-carrying vessels. The biggest I have ever seen off Sydney was about 30 metres long, at least 10 metres around, and trimmed of its branches.

It was floating with the north-to-south current just off Sydney Heads, and underneath it were thousands of small mahi-mahi (dolphin fish) and rat kingies up to 3 kilograms.

Marine biologist Dr Julian Pepperell tells me that all species of fish congregate under floating objects because they're a 'reference point in an otherwise featureless void'. In other words, it's like a dunny in the desert.

Dr Pepperell also believes that the shadows of debris and any ropes that may be attached to it provide cover in which fish hide. Because big fish eat smaller fish, the longer the log is in the water, the more it becomes an important part in the food chain for that area.

I'd often wondered what would congregate around a floating log in an area notorious for huge fish – such as off the Great Barrier Reef, where the predators have nicknames like 'the razor gang' and themselves get eaten by gamefish and sharks the size of which the brain cannot comprehend.

Well, a few years ago I got to find out, and if I live to be 1000 I doubt that I will ever see the likes of it again.

Fishing for black marlin with Captain Dennis 'Brazakka' Wallace off the No. 7 Ribbon Reef, about 145 kilometres north of Cairns and 72 kilometres out to sea, he spotted on the horizon what he thought was a life raft with three people on it. We pulled in the baits and steamed towards it.

It turned out to be the top 3 to 4 metres of a huge log which was sitting upright in the water – its diameter would have been the equivalent of a 10-man life raft. The water around it was crystal clear, but no matter how hard we gazed into it, there was just no end to that log. At a guess I would say it was 30 to 50 metres long.

This was the top 3 to 4 metres of a 50 metre log found floating out to sea. Around it was just about everything that swims, all feeding on each other.

And gathered around it was the largest congregation of big fish and sharks I have ever seen in my life. There were huge marlin, mahi-mahi, tuna, wahoo, mackerel, rainbow runners and heaps of whaler sharks. The first lure we cast at the tree was engulfed the second it hit the water, as the fish elbowed each other out of the way to get at it.

We would have caught a squillion fish if it wasn't for the predators. The minute something hooked up it was eaten by something bigger – either a mackerel, a wahoo or a shark. We watched in awe as a huge marlin swam among them and then disappeared into the abyss, obviously too full to bother hassling them.

After we'd had some fun, Brazakka put out a couple of big trolling lures and dragged them in a wide circle around the protruding log. The hook-up was almost instant, and as the big Shimano Tiagra reel yielded the 80 pound line to what was obviously a huge fish, we put first-time angler Steve Meads in the chair.

That big black marlin jumped all over the joint, and as it was Steve's first decent gamefish, we took it and weighed it – it was 350 kilograms. We hate killing them, but it's acceptable for an angler to take his first catch and then never kill another.

That log was just like an aquarium, and I'll probably never see anything like it again. It didn't look like a commercial log; Brazakka said it was probably thousands of years old and had possibly been uprooted and washed down the Amazon to somehow wind up as a fish haven in the Pacific. That day was an experience that will live with me all my life.

So what is there to learn from floating objects? They kill, and they provide life. Watch out for them ... and always look for the inevitable fish beneath them.

The Barra Boats

Next time you're hoeing into a delicious meal of wild barramundi in some toffy restaurant, spare a thought for the small brigade of tireless workers in Australia's north whose backbreaking task it is to make your meal possible.

Unlike the majority of our local table fish, wild barramundi are caught in the most remote places in the Top End of Australia. They have to be processed and snap frozen within hours of their capture so that they don't lose any of their delicious flavour or go off in the stifling heat.

From there the solid blocks of wild barramundi fillets are air-freighted from the nearest airport to fish wholesalers all over Australia; they eventually wind up on diners' plates in the most high-class restaurants in the country.

But the white plates, sparkling cutlery and fine wines of these places are a far cry from remote Holroyd Creek in western Cape York Peninsula, where the nearest restaurant is hundreds of kilometres away and the closest civilisation is the Edward River shop and post office, a mere three hours by dinghy and another three hours by car away.

These remote crocodile-infested waters are home to Dave and Beth Ward for most of the year. They live on their mothership-cum-processing plant at the creekside camp; their son Shane, who has his own mothership, deckie Shawn, and 21-year-old cook and barramundi filleter Seara Olsen, who's been working the barramundi boats since she was 14, share the camp. They net barra every day out of dories.

Beth and Dave have been living this nomadic existence for eight months of the year – from January to October – for the past 25 years. Both their son and daughter were raised and educated (by Beth) on the barra boats.

Beth and Dave plan on eventually retiring to their lush cattle property at Lakeland Downs, 80 kilometres southwest of Cooktown. That is where they spend the four months of the year that they aren't at the barra camp; they'll leave the whole barra operation to Shawn to run then. But they both readily admit that they'll miss the rugged lifestyle.

'We keep in touch with the outside world by satellite phone,' says Dave. 'And to be quite honest, we couldn't really give a damn what

The barra boat base is about as remote as any fishing enterprise could get.

The barra boats' crew with a batch of barramundi most anglers would die for.

goes on out there. It's all only misery and doom anyway. This is paradise, away from it all – none of us would give you two bob for the city.'

Dave, Shane and Shawn net the barramundi in an area up to 55 kilometres north and south of the Holroyd River. 'We get all sorts of fish in the nets,' says Shawn, who was originally from Sydney's western suburbs but is now a dinky-di Far North Queenslander. 'We get barramundi up to 25 kilograms, blue salmon, king salmon, and plenty of small whaler sharks, which we sell as flake. Today's catch is a pretty fair indication of a good mixed bag,' he said, pointing into the dories they use to clear the nets.

And a good catch it was. While I was there I watched them unload over a hundred barramundi (up to about 15 kilograms), an assortment of salmon and other estuary species and a few small sharks onto the mothership for cleaning.

'They think they do it tough, those blokes,' laughed Beth as the men unloaded the fish into the scuppers surrounding the filleting tables at

Dave Ward with the day's catch.

the back of the boat. She and Seara were putting a razor's edge on their filleting knives with the steel, preparing for the many hours of backbreaking work ahead.

'They get it too bloody easy – this is the real hard yakka, standing over the work bench and filleting the buggers,' she laughed as she took two perfect fillets off a 10 kilogram barramundi in a matter of seconds and flung them onto Seara's bench, where they were skinned and trimmed just as quickly and made ready for the freezer ... and eventually the top fish restaurants in the country.

So how do they cohabit with the crocodiles? 'We see them hanging around every day,' says Dave, 'but we've never had a real problem with them. Every now and then one will wander up into the camp, but that's pretty rare. As the wet season approaches, the waters rise, and they can swim further up onto the land. They come right into the camp then, which is a bit of a worry, but we're used to it.

'We used to throw the barramundi carcasses over the back of the boat, but in the end the crocs drove us nuts. Now we throw the frames back

186

into a dory, take 'em up around the corner into the creek and feed them to a family of wild pigs that Beth's almost got eating out of her hand.

'We used to fatten the pigs up then shoot 'em and sell 'em to one of the local crocodile farms, but these days it isn't worth it – they only fetch about 50 cents a kilo. You can't go lumpin' huge dead pigs around for that kind of money.'

I couldn't help myself; I had to ask the obvious question: 'Do you eat barramundi very often?' I asked, anticipating that they'd be sick to death of what us mugs pay an arm and a leg for.

'Of course we do,' they all chirped in unison. 'But not much lately – there are too many big, fat, succulent mud crabs around at the moment.'

I got the impression that the barra folk in that remote creek, which is about as far in the back-'o-beyond as you can get, were spoilt rotten. No pollution, no worries, no stress. Just plenty of hard work, fresh air, cold beer and barramundi and mud crabs galore.

What a life!

They'll Eat Anything

So you think fish are smart and very particular about their diets? The wily old bream? The cunning flathead? Wrong. Given the right circumstances, fish will eat anything, and the less likely the morsel, the more they seem to like it.

A popular urban myth told time and again is the one about how some gangsters threw an unfaithful associate in the drink and then attracted the sharks to him by pouring buckets of bullock's blood into the water.

Not true. Yes, I know you've heard it in one form or another before and you believe it to be true, but I'm here to tell you that it's a load of bullock's – so to speak.

Why? Simple. Under normal circumstances sharks are not attracted to land-animal blood, and that's that. Mind you, that's not to say that they couldn't become fond of it if there were an abattoir pumping blood and animal offal into the ocean on a permanent basis. But land-based animals are not really on a shark's diet ... at least not the way fish, whales, seals, dolphins and other sea creatures are.

Remember the dog that went missing in the water in *Jaws*? As factually absurd as *Jaws* was, that was one of the only true bits. There were some other preposterous blunders, like this next little gem.

Remember the ill-fated Captain Quint (Robert Shaw) sitting in the cabin telling Richard Dreyfuss and Roy Scheider how he survived the sinking of the USS *Indianapolis* in 1945?

'We was returnin' to Pearl Harbor after deliverin' the bomb when we was torpedoed. The *Indianapolis* sank within minutes,' Quint recalled in American/Irish drawl. 'Seein' as our mission was top secret, no one knew our predicament. Eight hundred of us took to the water, and after four days and five nights, when help finally arrived, only 200 of us survived. The rest were eaten by the sharks.'

Absolute crap. History books tell us that on the fateful day when the *Indianapolis* went down, almost 500 men perished in the water – by drowning, dehydration or whatever – but only 60 to 80 of them were actually taken by sharks.

That, and the fact that white pointers don't stalk humans the way the critter (with the IQ of a brain surgeon!) in all the *Jaws* movies did, are possibly the two greatest lies about sharks ever laid on a gullible public.

But back to the plot. Yes, sharks do eat dogs. That bit is true. They eat dogs regularly, but not usually in the surf; it is more common upriver, where the water is murky and in the dimness a paddling dog looks like something a shark would like to eat.

And the sharks that eat them are not white pointers, because white pointers are an oceanic species. They are almost certainly bull whalers that swim far into the upper reaches of estuaries in search of a quick snack.

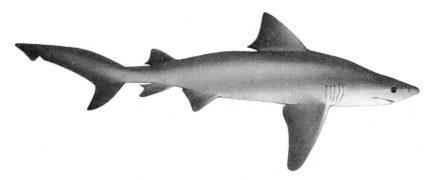

The deadly bull shark is rather partial to eating swimming dogs.

So where is all this leading us? Let me explain. What I'm trying to say is that sea creatures don't usually eat anything out of their environment; the bullock's blood myth is a classic example. However, as I said earlier, there are exceptions to every rule.

One of the favourite all-time baits for bream is a mixture of cheese, salami and bread dough, all kneaded up into a 'pudding' mix and stuck onto the hook rather than threaded on. Not much else except the bream will touch it, and I can only wonder where the hell a bream would acquire a taste for such a concoction – worse still, who was the inventor?

Even if you had just been sentenced to 10 terms of life imprisonment and you had all that time to come up with a ridiculous bait for bream, I doubt you'd suggest that one, so whoever first put it together is one bizarre individual.

Bream are also suckers for a bit of rump steak, and I can recall times in my youth when they wouldn't touch anything else. Mum used to get pretty cranky when she'd get home and that night's roast was gone from the fridge, but we usually brought home a feed of fish that more than compensated.

We never stopped to wonder why those bream in Perth's Swan River would prefer the unnatural red meat to fish strips and prawns. It wasn't until years later that I realised that we used to fish just upstream from the Acme Smallgoods factory; while we never actually saw the waste meat being pumped into the river through the outlet pipes, we certainly found plenty in the bream's stomachs when we cleaned them after the day's fishing. So that explained that.

But it doesn't explain why some trout prefer kernels of corn to juicy grasshoppers. Now that's a worry: who on Earth was the person who first put corn on a hook and discovered that the trout can't help themselves?

And while on the subject of strange things catching fish, it's interesting to note that the most successful trolling lure ever made is the humble Japanese feather jig, which is made from – you may have guessed it – chicken feathers. And just in case you're thinking that the tailor, salmon, kingfish, mackerel, tuna and other creatures that maraud on the surface are into a bit of tail-feather, think again.

The fact that the lure is made of feathers has a lot to do with its success, but only because when the lure is pulled at any sort of speed behind a boat, the feathers tuck in behind the metal head and flatten out to resemble a scurrying baitfish, most likely a pilchard, whitebait, bluebait or garfish, to a pursuing predator.

And while the mighty kingfish may well lay claim to being pound for pound the toughest fighter of them all in Australian waters, the old kingie and its almost identical closest relative, the samson fish, are total boofheads when it comes to munching on something they shouldn't. Well, maybe it's not that they shouldn't be; it's more that it's something you wouldn't expect them to eat – chromed metal jigs.

The rules in Kingfishville are that if one does it, then it's OK for all of them to do it. Just like lemmings. One jumps off the cliff and the other wombats follow. For this reason it is easier to catch kingfish by dropping a flashing metal lure down into their domain, be it a reef or an undersea mountain, then winding and dropping it at a rapid pace until one of the drongos eats it. You know that all the others will do the same the next time the lure comes down.

It's called jigging – or if you're doing it way offshore, deep-jigging – and the kingies are suckers for it every time. Albert Einsteins in the last life they were not. Considering that most modern lures are made of either wood or plastic, and that the olden-day lures were made of bone, it's not hard to see that fish aren't too fussy when it comes to eating.

In the circumstances that led to what became known as the Shark Arm Murder in 1935, a captured tiger shark chundered up a human arm.

So let's look at the assortment of tasty tidbits we know they eat: dogs, animal meat, cheese, salami, dough, metal, chicken feathers, wood, plastic, corn and human body parts.

And some of you folk out there have the hide to think fish are smart. The wily old bream. The cunning old kingie. As smart as a marlin.

I don't think so. Just keep catching 'em and letting 'em go. Anything that silly deserves to be caught more than once.

Tacklin' Tassie's Tuna

Of all the great fishing holes in Australia, Tasmania takes a lot of beating. It's got the scenery, the fish, and the Tasmanians are a delight … nothing seems to faze them in the least. And that includes their extraordinary weather, which can be bitter one minute and boiling the next. And the rougher it gets, the more they like their fishing …

They've got a saying in southeast Tasmania that goes like this: 'Tassie has four distinct seasons. Trouble is, you get 'em all in one day.' I was invited down to Tassie a few years back to do a story on the Australian Bluefin Tuna Championships, put on by the Tuna Club of Tasmania, and believe me, the locals fish in mountainous seas and howling winds that would make us mainlanders throw the alarm clock at the wall, roll over and go back to sleep.

Then, in the twinkling of an eye, the sun's out, the wind drops and the seas flatten to millpond conditions. It was a weird experience putting my head down for a short nap in the middle of a howling gale and waking up a few minutes later in perfect conditions, wondering if I hadn't dreamt it all. The locals take it all in their stride and reckon 'city folk' like me will never get used to it. They're dead right.

But weird fishing conditions or not, I wouldn't miss an opportunity to fish Tassie, because what some spots might lack in fish they certainly make up for in scenery and hospitality that's darn near impossible to beat.

Forget all that rubbish about Tasmanians having two heads and being a bunch of country hicks. That may apply in some areas, the same as it does up here on the mainland, but for my money the Tasmanians are the friendliest and most hospitable people you're ever likely to meet.

So when Ron Di Felice from Tasmanian Tourism rang and asked if I'd like to be their guest at the Bluefin Championships, I didn't hesitate. I'd never been bluewater fishing in Tassie before, so the message on the bottom of Ronnie's fax that said, 'You will have a great time experiencing our crazy fishing style' went straight over the top of my head. Boy, was I in for a giant surprise.

The competition is held out of Eaglehawk Neck, a small fishing village about an hour's drive south of Hobart. Ron had arranged accommodation for me at the local hotel, which overlooked glorious Pirate's Bay.

The following morning, at 6 am, I stuck my head out the window for a weather check and had my hair flattened by a 'breeze' that was the equivalent of standing behind a jumbo jet on take-off. 'They'll call it off for sure,' I said to myself as I slid back into the warmth and pulled the doona over my head. This thought was short-lived.

'Come on, mate, they're all waiting for you at the wharf,' Ronnie called as he pounded on my door to wake me up. 'We'll get some tuna today for sure. The weather's perfect for it.'

Maybe I'd been dreaming about the weather being so crook. I stuck my head out again for a second opinion. Ouch! It was like someone stabbing me in the face with frozen needles. The 'breeze' had picked up enough speed to blow a sailor off your sister.

'You've brought the good weather with you,' Captain Gerald Spalding told me as he gunned his magnificent 17 metre Randall-hulled charter boat, the *Norseman III*, through a 6 metre wave.

The Bottom End Boys with one of the many southern bluefin tuna caught during the competition.

'The last couple of days the weather's been lousy. The sun was out, there was hardly any breeze and the seas were as flat as a lizard drinkin'. We've been waitin' for this change. We need a little bit of activity on the surface to bring the bluefin up.'

A little bit of activity on the surface! As big and heavy as *Norseman III* was, she was all over the joint like a matchstick in a washing machine. I looked around for a bit of sympathy.

'Terrific conditions,' I said as a joke to Rob Richardson, one of our fishing team. 'Yeah, she's a beauty,' he replied. 'Looks like you brought the good weather with you from the big smoke. With a bit of luck, the wind might pick up a bit to gale force ... but that's really asking too much.'

I'd died and gone to fisherman's hell. I looked around at the rest of the team: Rino De Santo, Paul Williams, Anthony Whitbread and deckie John Rooke. The 'Bottom End Boys', they call themselves. They were all grinning from ear to ear, like a gang of carpet snakes that had just crawled out of a chicken house.

'Seein' as you're on board, Gerald's going to take us out to the Continental Shelf as a special treat,' John explained. 'And just before the Shelf there's a big hole – about the size of a couple of football fields – and on these good days the waves can get up to 10 metres in there.

'He must have taken an instant liking to you, because he only takes special people to the Hole, so act surprised when we hit it and let him tell you all about it himself. You'll know when we're there. The boat will nearly capsize when the first big greenie hits us.'

I couldn't wait. And to celebrate our journey into aquatic hell and (I hoped) back, my new chums offered me cold beers, pickled onions and spicy salami and cheese sambos. I thought I was going to throw up for the first time in 40 years of going to sea.

When I asked where the raft and lifejackets were, they explained to me not to worry about them, because if the boat sank she had a watertight compartment up front and it was better to cling to the nose of the boat as it stuck out of the water than to try to make it to any nearby islands and be pounded to death on the rocks.

I was so pleased I'd asked.

We were in the Hole, rising and falling about 8 metres, when the first tuna struck. Our angler pulled the lure out of its mouth, mercifully, and it escaped.

'Bloody shame we lost that fish,' Gerald cursed. 'I love backin' the boat up on them tuna in here in the Hole on these good days. It gives the crew a chance to get a good look at the hull of the boat when she's right out of the water, so they can let me know if it needs a clean or not.'

He seemed a little disappointed when I crashed on the divan in the cabin just as we were passing through the second football field. When I awoke about an hour later it was eerie. Everything was different. I could actually hear the engine noises over the crashing of the waves. In fact there were no waves. The boat wasn't pitching and rolling, and the crew were dead silent. The gusting wind and pitching seas had been replaced by blinding rain and lightning. And the sun was shining.

Gerald was really upset. 'That bloody beaut weather was only a squall,' he grizzled. 'And now we're gettin' the lousy weather back, bugger it. Just look at it. Almost flat seas and the sun shining. But at least we've got some rain and lightning with it.'

Terrific. Imagine getting through the day without rain and lightning. What a bummer. All the anglers also seemed depressed that the gale had subsided, and when we returned home fishless they prayed for 'good' weather the next day.

'We'll just have to make the most of it,' Ronnie said when he picked me up at the hotel in the dark of the following morning. 'The winds will only be gusting up to about 40 knots, and the sea isn't going to get much better than a 4 metre swell.'

Gerald was a little more enthusiastic. 'Great day for showin' you around,' he said as *Norseman III* broached under a side-on 5 metre wall of green water a few minutes after we left the wharf at Fortescue Bay. He pointed at a giant rock formation sticking out of the ocean ahead of us like Cleopatra's Needle.

'That's the Big Hippolite,' he enthused. 'On a good tuna day the waves break over the top of her and you can't see her at all.' I couldn't wait to get out there on a good tuna day. The Big Hippolite was at least 30 metres tall.

As our next sightseeing spot was Tasman Island, a few kilometres to the south, we had the wind, rain, fog patches and huge waves coming at us side-on while we trolled half a dozen lures through the thick of it – most of them spent more time out of the water than in it.

And just when I was feeling crook for the second time in 40 years of going to sea, we got a solid strike. The boys got their rods in and out of the road and let Ronnie play what was obviously a big and powerful bluefin tuna.

After a 15 minute battle on 15 kilogram line, Ronnie had the 25 kilogram tuna alongside, and I got my first good look at what the Japanese pay up to $200 a kilo for – they eat it raw, as sushi and sashimi. And what a beautiful fish. Short, stocky and built like a guided missile. Designed to hunt and kill.

The boys were optimistic about catching more, but all of a sudden the

weather deteriorated something shocking. The wind dropped off, the sun came out, and the seas abated to a leisurely swell.

'I must have run over a bloody Chinaman,' Gerald cursed. 'Just when I find the spot, the weather turns lousy. Let's pray for some great weather tomorrow. In the meantime I'll show you Tasman Island, one of the highlights of the trip south.'

Tasman Island – with its only highlight, the lighthouse – must be the bleakest, most isolated, miserable place I've ever laid eyes on, though clearly my hosts love it. It's worth the trip, but you wouldn't want to live there.

And so, with that one fish in the boat, plus a couple the boys had caught the day before I arrived, *Norseman III* hit the front of the competition with a day to go. Could they hang on to win the most coveted trophy of them all, Champion Boat?

I didn't get much sleep that night because the wind was trying to rip the roof off the pub to let the torrential rain in. Good. They would cancel the day's fishing and my new friends would become Champion Boat.

With yesterday's fish I had my story and pictures and everyone was happy. Finally my broken sleep was interrupted by Ronnie pounding on the door.

'Mate, let's get moving,' he yelled through the door. 'We've got perfect tuna weather and Gerald's got the gun deckie comin' down all the way from northern Tassie. If you ever want to see some action, today's the day.'

I tried not to even contemplate what it was going to be like out in the boat. Just the drive to the wharf took an extra 10 minutes because we were driving into the

Bert, the gun deckie from the north.

wind. I tried to get out of going by explaining that I had a bad case of terminal dandruff, but there was no way this lot were going to let me escape.

Gerald was drooling and salivating out of the corner of his mouth like Sir Les Patterson when he's full of the turps. 'She's a bottler,' he enthused, rubbing his frozen hands together with glee. 'Perfect tuna weather. The wind's from the southeast at 50 knots and gusting to about 70. And the seas could be as high as 10 metres. You'll see it all today.'

As I attempted to flee down the gangplank in the direction of the hotel and my warm bed, Gerald grabbed me by my shirt collar, yanked me back on board and introduced me to the gun deckie from the north. 'Bert, say g'day to the fishin' and writin' photographic journalist from the mainland.

'Paul, Bert drove all through the night in blinding rain and fog to be here, 'cause he can sniff a tuna day a million miles away. Can't you, Bert? And he's gonna get us a bunch of 'em.'

Bert shook my hand vigorously, and smiled a huge toothless smile through the red beard that covered most of his face – that said it all.

Today was indeed a tuna day.

As we rounded the corner it was like staring death straight in the face. It was like the end of the world. Armageddon. The conflict between the forces of good and evil on the battlefield of the Apocalypse. The sky was black and the rain pounded huge seas that had been whipped up by the gale-force winds.

And it was indeed a tuna day. The boys caught three whoppers, each somewhere near 30 kilograms – and lost a couple more because of the appalling conditions – and the gun deckie from the north was pretty to watch. The boys took out Champion Boat, Champion Team and a swag of other goodies.

And me? I was so wobbly on my pins that I closed my eyes under the shower that night and fell over. Would I do it again? As much as I've complained, I'd have to say yes. A day out with the Bottom End Boys is worth the punishment ... from both the sea and from them.

Sir Adrian's Record

This story is widely accepted as true and is often repeated in legal circles. It was first told by Sir Adrian himself, one night when he was flyblown, and he deeply regrets telling it. Names have been changed for obvious reasons.

Chief Magistrate Sir Adrian Farrington-Roycroft, OBE, was over the moon. The first day out on his brand new game boat *Quay Witness* and he had christened it with a whopper blue marlin – his first. And to top it all off, it could be an Australian record.

He held his breath as the huge fish was hauled up on the scales.

The crowd gasped as the weighmaster called it ... 'It's 238 kilograms on 15 kilogram line. Congratulations, Sir Adrian. A new Australian record claim on 15 kilogram line.'

He yelled it loud enough for the crowd to hear. Might as well slime the old prick, he thought to himself, you never know when you might have to front him on a drink-drive – and on such acts of antisocial behaviour involving alcohol, Sir Adrian was known to be merciless.

Everyone adjourned to the bar of the Sydney Game Fishing Club, where the drinks were on Sir Adrian. They all knew his reputation as a wowser but today he surprised them all by his presence in a room where the dreaded drink was being served. And he was paying for it!

Sir Adrian's moral crusades were legendary. He made Mother Teresa look like Charles Manson. Everything even halfway acceptable he hated – pornography, abortion, pot, prostitution – but most of all he hated alcohol.

It was this platform, along with a lot of arse-licking, that had brought him to the pinnacle of his profession: he was the most respected district court magistrate in the country.

But Sir Adrian had a deep, dark secret. He was a closet piss-head. And a cunning one at that. Exposure could ruin him, and over the years he had developed a technique that allowed him to join in the fun without anyone being any the wiser.

He would wait until everyone around him was half flyblown and then start topping up his customary Coca-Cola with Scotch from one of his many hip flasks. No one ever knew.

He saved his secret piss-ups for the right occasion – maybe a birthday or a lodge night. And today was such an occasion – his first marlin and an Australian record to boot.

And so the festivities progressed into the night. Eventually until Sir Adrian got paralytic and collapsed behind the big leather couch next to the trophy case.

When it was time to go his fellow drinkers let him sleep on. They felt it was not a good idea to wake him – he would then know they were on to him and he could make life difficult.

Instead, they moved him from full view; they would later pretend that they hadn't seen him anywhere, saying they thought he had snuck off home.

Of course he would agree that he had – 'Couldn't stand all that boozing, you know!'

Sir Adrian awoke to a dark, deserted clubhouse. He turned on the lights and found, to his horror, that he had chundered all over himself.

He looked like a mobile pizza and smelled like a brewery horse fart. At least he had sobered up. But what to do? He wandered up the road and eventually hailed a cab that would take him as he was.

On the way to his city penthouse he plotted his excuse for the dreaded Lady Farrington-Roycroft, the Methodist minister's daughter he had been stuck with for the past 40 years.

He knew she suspected that he had the odd nip, but even after all those years together she had never been able to prove anything.

Tonight would be the ultimate test.

'Sorry I'm late, darling,' he purred as the dragon came to the door, curious as to his whereabouts.

'Had a bit of drama on the way home.'

'Really,' she said suspiciously.

He explained about the big fish and shouting for the bar.

The old anaconda hissed at the thought of wasting their good money on the demon drink.

He then told her that the chap who offered him a lift home had appeared a little intoxicated, and rather than be put in a compromising position should they be pulled over, he had elected to leave early and catch a cab.

'Coming down Oxford Street,' he explained, 'we were stopped at the lights and this drunk lunged at the cab, put his head in the window and vomited all over me,' he said.

'Fortunately the cab driver recognised me, apprehended the drunk and the police have him locked up at Darlinghurst police station. I've made sure he'll come before me tomorrow and I'm going to give him three months in Long Bay Jail.

'Now, my darling, do you mind if I get out of these filthy clothes and go to bed? I'm absolutely exhausted after catching that huge fish.'

She smiled proudly at her husband and prepared him a hot bath.

The following morning Sir Adrian was resting in his chambers nursing a monumental hangover when the phone rang. It was Lady Farrington-Roycroft.

'Sir Adrian,' she chortled. 'Remember that drunk who vomited all over you last night? What are you going to do about him?'

'They're bringing him up from the cells right now,' he replied. 'He appears before me at 10 am and I'm going to give him three months in the Bay.

'You'd better make it six,' she said. 'Because he shit in your underpants, too!'

The Topless Shark

Prospects for gamefishing didn't look too bright that first Sunday in November as Pam Hudspeth and Jack Farrell headed north towards Long Reef. The discussion was not about how many fish they would catch; it was about how long it would be before the elements would drive them back to the comforts of the Rose Bay Marina. The 15 knot nor'-easter made for unpleasant conditions aboard Pam's 7.5 metre Winamee II.

Mooring at Long Reef was not without its hazards – the raging 3 knot current to the south and the joggling, choppy conditions combined to make the task much tougher than usual. With the reef pick securely fastened, they set about preparing rigs for sharks and kingfish.

There's never much doing in November, so the team decided to fish with light line, to get as much sport as possible from the few predators. A rod and reel fitted with 15 kilogram test line was baited with a 3 kilogram kingfish and lowered to the bottom with hopes of finding a shark. The other lines were set just below the surface, aimed at migratory yellowfin tuna.

By 11 am Jack Farrell was just about ready to call it a day, but suddenly the ratchet on the 15 kilogram outfit went off, indicating that something was interested in the kingie. Jack was to take first strike of the day, so with the rod butt secured in the rod bucket, he wound up the clutch and struck hard, hoping the hook would penetrate deeply.

Anticipating a common grey nurse, Jack was surprised when the fish peeled line from the reel as it felt the hook, didn't like it, and headed for New Zealand, about 2000 kilometres and a few weeks' swimming away.

After about 20 minutes, Jack was able to turn the fish and bring it to within about 15 metres of the boat – close, but not close enough to identify it. He tightened the drag to the limit, but the added strain only caused the fish to start circling the boat.

After several hair-raising trips to the bow of the boat to pass the rod and reel between the mooring rope and vessel, Pam climbed up the flying bridge to get a better look at their adversary. 'It's a tiger, Jack – and it's a big one,' Pam yelled.

This surprised both Jack and Pam. Tiger sharks were not rare, but they were certainly unusual this early in the season. You can never tell whether these out-of-season fish are really early arrivals or leftovers from the previous season.

Still the circling continued – two hours of backbreaking angling. During that time Jack must have gone around the boat at least 50 times, each time having to pass the rod and reel under the anchor rope, which only added to the physical torture.

During all this, the shark ventured no further than 45 metres from the boat. They decided to tie the anchor rope off to a buoy and chase the fish. They would then come back later for the anchor rope.

It was almost as though the fish knew the chase was on: it headed east at breakneck speed with Jack and Pam churning through the rough seas in hot pursuit. It took an hour for the pursuit tactics to pay off. At last the 5 metres of double line appeared above the surface, with the wire trace almost within reach.

Had they had another hand on the boat, the shark would have been theirs. But Jack couldn't hold the fish in position long enough for Pam to come down from the flying bridge and take a wrap on the wire.

The topless shark.

They had to watch as the shark took off again, undoubtedly shaken by being so close to the boat. Fifty, 100, then 200 metres of line disappeared from the reel as Pam headed the boat after their quarry again.

Now they had time to get their bearings. They were about 5 kilometres south of their original position, just off Sydney Heads.

Then the incredible happened. The tiger turned a quick 180 degrees and made a beeline directly for North Head, or, to be more precise, straight towards Sydney Harbour. Naturally this suited Jack and Pam down to the ground – the nasty conditions were behind them now, and the only bit of discomfort occurred when they would occasionally turn side-on to get a better angle at the fish.

By the time they were approaching North Head they were joined by Jack Paton on *Signa*. He stayed close by for an hour before proceeding to the Watsons Bay weigh station to let them know that *Winamee II* was on to a good fish and to have the scales in readiness should all go well. *Signa* also arranged radio contact with them every hour on the hour. Now that they were organised, Jack and Pam thought they could relax a little.

As they came closer to the cliffs, the backwash of the waves started to toss the boat about vigorously. Jack had to use all his skill to prevent a bust-off. Still on almost full drag, Jack couldn't get that fish any closer than about 6 metres.

If they'd thought they had troubles before, they should have had a peek at what was around the corner! The raging flood tide from the recent heavy rains was trying to force the boat back to the east, and now the fish was 'bogging' into the flood tide, in typical tiger fashion, obviously thinking that he was nosing into a fast current.

To add further to their woes, the shark was heading straight for the shipping lanes, at incredible speed, and now, with the sun shining, the harbour was a hive of activity. First a pleasure cruiser, then a Japanese tuna boat and next, believe it or not, a submarine, all came within spitting distance of cutting the line.

To add to this already comical situation, they had to put up with sirens blaring and hooters hooting – some from well-wishers, but most from irate skippers who were being forced off course. What the hell! Pam did her job and navigated that whole amazing act right through the middle of the flotilla and towards Camp Cove beach. At the time, Camp Cove was a topless bathing beach.

So there they were, the world's unluckiest shark navigating the boat towards a topless beach, followed by a fleet of onlookers.

As *Winamee II* approached the beach it became obvious to the semi-nude bathers that this was no minuscule creature they were chasing. With much shrieking and boob-clutching, there was a mass exodus of scantily clad beauties – to the enormous delight of the male onlookers.

About now the shark eased down, and Jack could feel the last of the double line slip through his fingers and onto the reel. He shouted to Pam to leave the boat slowly idling ahead and to rush down and take the trace, so that she could get the huge flying head gaff into position.

Pam's first hit with the big flyer was perfectly placed, in the tougher section of the fish's underbelly. As another flyer went in and the shark tried to eat the marlin board – and decapitate Jack with its tail – the crowd went berserk. Not a nipple moved from the beach until the tail rope was secured. Amid much jubilation, our heroes headed for the weigh station at Watsons Bay. The six hour ordeal was over – well, for Jack and Pam, at least.

To this day, some of those topless ladies are still convinced that that whopper tiger shark was caught right where they gaffed it. And mothers always talk to their daughters – that's why even today you rarely see the nubiles venture into the water at Camp Cove.

The Dark Side of Fishing Knives

*Fishing knives are among the most lethal legal
implements ever invented. I've lost count of the number of
accidents I'm aware of that have been caused by them —
on a boat or just in the normal course of a day's fishing.*

There are no legal requirements or regulations controlling fishing knives, simply because it would be impossible to enforce them. It's stupid to even contemplate regulating fishing knives; the only sensible approach is to educate people about how to avoid coming to grief with one.

For these and many other reasons, fishing knives also have many infamous places in history, but none of these incidents relates to cutting up fish or fishing line. I would bet that more accidents are caused by fishing knives than any other ten fishing implements combined — discounting the odd fish hook in the flesh, that is.

Legitimate accidents, I'm talking about. Not premeditated ones. While we're on that subject, let's take a quick squiz at a few famous fishing knife incidents that I can assure you were no accident.

In 1961, mild-mannered mail sorter William McDonald walked into Mick Simmons Sports Store in Sydney's Haymarket and brought a fishing knife, explaining to the sales assistant that he was going to try his luck around Sydney Harbour.

It's a pity that Bill McDonald didn't tell the sales assistant what he was going to try his luck at … it could have saved a few lives.

Bill's specialty was stabbing derelicts to death with his 'fishing knife'. When bodies covered from head to toe in stab wounds started turning up all over Sydney, the killer became known as 'the Mutilator', and Sydney was under lock and key every night until William McDonald was eventually apprehended and thrown into jail, where he remains to this day. How's that for a fishing knife story?

And I suppose we can only wonder if Mick 'Crocodile' Dundee would have roamed off into the sunset with his beautiful young New York lady reporter friend if it wasn't for the fishing knife that he plunged into the noggin of the giant croc that almost ate her as she bathed beside the billabong.

What's that? It wasn't a fishing knife? Yes it was. *We* all know that Mick used it for skinning crocs, but as killing crocs, let alone selling their skins, is illegal, he called it his 'fishing' knife and no one was any the wiser.

And if the writers of Crocodile Dundee had written the truth, it would have changed one of the great movie one-liners of all time. It would have gone like this: 'That's not a fishing knife. *This* is a fishing knife.' No way, that sounds terrible. Thank God they didn't change it. It's much better the way it is.

And then there was the tragic incident a few years ago that began with a young man minding his own business fishing for bream on Sydney's Coogee Beach.

A young teacher was conducting a high school excursion nearby. A couple of the schoolboys snuck off and went through the fisherman's bag, removing several articles, including his car keys.

The altercation that followed resulted in the teacher dying from a single stab wound to the chest from the man's fishing knife. The young fisherman was eventually tried, convicted of manslaughter and sent to prison.

More recently, in March 2000, in Western Australia, veterinary hospital receptionist Kelly Fuller stabbed schoolgirl Jessica Lang

47 times with her father's fishing knife after her (Kelly's) boyfriend, disc jockey Myk Bloom, dumped her for Lang.

Blind Freddie will tell you that fishing knives come in all shapes and sizes and that most tackle boxes and boats carry at least a couple. The most popular ones are the general purpose model, which has a thick blade, a blade guard, and a scaler on the back, and the narrow-bladed filleting knife, which is vital for cleaning your catch on the spot and taking home the fillets.

The two best tips I can give you on fishing knives are that they should be kept in the sheath or similar safety cover at all times, and that they must be kept sharp.

A blunt knife is five times more dangerous than a sharp one. Why? With a blunt knife you try a lot harder. If you are filleting a fish and the knife isn't sharp and is cutting roughly, you tend to lean on it a little bit more; chances are you'll end up with it in some part of your body, particularly if you fillet the way most people do – with the blade going towards you.

Blunt knives also tend to get rusty, and if they do happen to inflict a wound on you, the chances of you catching some horrible disease like tetanus are high. Try to imagine the beautiful little germ traps on a rust- and muck-encrusted fishing knife. Then imagine it going into your flesh. Yuk. So keep it clean and sharp and rust-free. And always remember to fillet *away* from your body.

Also remember that the fish you intend to take home for dinner deserve to die with dignity – a razor-sharp knife will see to it that their throats are cut swiftly and cleanly, with the minimum amount of cruelty.

During my years on boats I've seen people sit on fishing knives, fall on them, grab the blades, slice their fingers off with them and accidentally stab themselves and others with them. The smartest move you'll ever make is to see to it that your fishing knives are in their sheaths at all times rather than just lying around on the rocks or bait board on the boat.

Remember, all fishing knives have points – very, very pointed points,

A selection of fishing knives. But remember – they can be deadly.

designed to penetrate tough skin and bone. They are meant to cut through skulls and tails and scales and fins and beaks, so just about any part of the human anatomy is a piece of cake for them.

If you can use one, a butcher's steel is perfect for keeping a fine edge on the blade. The go is to sharpen the knife on a stone when you first get the knife, then just tickle it sharp with the butcher's steel when it looks and feels as though it's going blunt.

Files are useless for on-the-spot sharpening, as is a sharpening stone – leave it in the workshop at home, because it takes forever to sharpen a knife on one, particularly at sea. Remember what you're out there for: to fish, not sharpen knives. That's a home job.

After a series of nasty accidents involving knives on a boat I crewed on for a couple of seasons, we all went and brought one of those multi-purpose pocket knives. I'm sure you know the ones I mean. They are like a Swiss Army knife but without all the gadgets. They just have things that are applicable to fishing – fold-up blades, scissors, wire-cutters, pliers – and they retail for $80–$120.

Each of us carried one of these for cutting wire, nylon and all the dozens of other little things you need a fishing knife for. When we needed to fillet a fish or cut through bone or skin on a big fish, we'd get out the knife designed specifically for that.

No more accidents. Oh, one last thing. If you're walking around with your big fishing knife in your belt rather than in your tackle box, you'll be charged with carrying a lethal weapon. Because outside the things that fishing knives were designed for, that's exactly what they are.

The Deep Sea Contract

I have fished with many famous and notorious people over the years, and of them all, I loved the notorious gangster Theo the Boss the most. As sinister as he was to the rest of the world, Theo was always good to me, and he was my friend. Although I have changed some of the names and the circumstances slightly, this is a true story.

I will never forget that day as long as I live. We were fishing off Sydney for sharks on Theo the Boss's 56 foot Hatteras gamefishing boat *Saint Theodore*. But believe me, Theo was no saint. He was a card-carrying member of organised crime and had every Sydney politician and cop in his pocket. Theo the Boss was 'the Man'.

And only now that Theo is pushing up daisies can I tell this story.

Through the 1960s and 1970s Theo the Boss ran Sydney's biggest illegal casino, the Nugget Club, without fear of reprimand. Collecting bad debts and rubbing shoulders with racketeers, standover men and hired killers was all in a night's work.

And the Boss had them all terrified. He was a proper gangster, straight out of a 1930s movie. If there were an Edward G. Robinson look-alike competition, Theo the Boss would have come first, third and ninth.

A short, stocky Greek with a patent-leather haircut and pencil-thin mustache, Theo dressed the part, in double-breasted Raymond Peraggio handmade suits, gaudy silk ties and spit-polished black-and-white or brown-and-white Mellers shoes. He wore a diamond the size of a duck egg on the small finger of his left hand, smoked huge Cuban cigars and drank only the finest Scotch whisky.

The Boss was chauffeur-driven around town by his ever-present henchman, Gringo, in a huge black Mark V four-door Lincoln Continental Town Car with pitch-black windows. The Mafia Staff Car, the boys called it.

Gringo carried the biggest gun I have ever seen in my life, and if anyone suspicious came within cooee of the Boss he would produce it. If the need arose, he would use it first and ask questions later.

Being offside with the Boss was not a good place to be. But if you were his friend, he was the best bloke in the world and couldn't do enough for you. Money was no object – he would spray his clan with the best of everything. To me, the Boss was a beaut bloke. I crewed for him on *Saint Theodore* and I was his friend.

The Boss's two great passions were swearing and fishing – in that order. And he didn't give a shit who he dropped the magic word in front of. In a twenty-word sentence, eighteen would be swearwords. And with the Boss's thick accent and sinister delivery, it was hilarious to hear him unleash a mouthful on someone and reduce them to a gibbering mess. Mind you, none of us ever laughed to his face.

Whenever he could, the Boss would escape the art deco decor and the hustle and bustle of the Nugget Club and go fishing on his magnificent *Saint Theodore*, which was the apple of his eye.

His pride and joy had every possible extra, and the boss's minions kept her like a new pin. We even had to take our deck shoes off before we walked inside the main saloon. To do anything against *Saint Theodore* was to put your life in very grave danger.

'Paul B, you bloody fuckin' bastard. You like fuckin' fishin' on my bloody fuckin' beauty bastard boat?' Theo would always ask me as he sat back in his giant leather lounge chair chewing on a mammoth Monte

Cristo and sucking on a vase of 20-year-old Chivas Regal as we headed out to the fishing grounds many miles off the Sydney coastline at around 7 am.

'Absolutely, Theo,' I would always reply. 'Fishing on the best boat in the country with you is always fun. There's certainly never a dull moment.' And it was the truth.

Gringo would always analyse what I had said, his dull brain trying to figure out whether or not I was taking the piss out of the Boss and whether or not he would need to tug my coat. He never had to.

Cutting into the nicotine and alcohol at dawn was perfectly normal to Theo. After all, he'd been up all night running his gambling house, then counting money into the small hours of the morning; to Theo and his henchman it was just like going to the pub at five o'clock after a hard day's work, except that we were heading out in search of giant gamefish instead.

Curiously, Theo the Boss didn't do much big gamefishing himself, preferring to hand-line for snapper, or 'snappers', as he called them. So every second Sunday we would fish for snappers and every other Sunday we would fish the point-scoring competition for marlin, tuna and sharks for the Sydney Game Fishing Club. And we did extremely well.

Our crew consisted of the legendary Watsons Bay boatman Jack Farrell, the Boss's son Nicky, Gringo and myself. Jack was in his early seventies and had gaffed countless world records for most of the big names in gamefishing. There wasn't much old Jack didn't know about bluewater fishing.

The Boss and Jack got on like a house on fire. They were about the same age and the Boss didn't have to put on any of that gangster bullshit with Jack. They would just sit and talk about fishing over a fine old Scotch. Jack wasn't in the least bit interested in what the Boss did for a quid and seemed totally oblivious to the fact that he was the fishing master for the heaviest mobster in Sydney, probably Australia.

Theo's son Nicky was a terrific bloke in his early thirties who had no interest whatever in following in the family tradition – he was content to run his small law practice, which specialised in conveyancing.

Nicky loved anything to do with boats and fishing; he drove the boat while Jack and I looked after the gear and rigged the baits. We took it in turns to catch the marlin, sharks and tuna – the Boss didn't care if he caught a gamefish or not. As long as he did some hand-lining for the snappers, he was happy.

The Boss often entertained characters that we had only seen photos of and articles about in the papers. They would huddle and whisper in the saloon of the boat with the door closed, drinking whisky amid a fog of expensive blue cigar smoke.

'Don't you take any notice of what you see or hear in there, young fella,' wise old Jack would whisper to me as we rigged the baits and set the lines. 'Fishermen live a lot longer than gangsters.'

Gringo always came along for the ride. He looked out of place at sea with his fedora sloped down over his eyes and the huge cannon bulging in his jacket, but it was his job to see that the Boss came to no harm, no matter where he was.

This day we were berleying and drifting the Twelve Mile Reef with big surface baits for sharks. It was mid-August and the seas were flat, with a lazy roll from the south. August is mako shark time and they are

The big mako hung around the back of the boat, chewing on the berley pot and making a bloody pest of himself.

the meanest, most unpredictable critters that swim. Makos twist and turn in the gaff ropes and often jump into the boat with their jaws snapping ferociously – anything that gets in the way gets badly bitten. It is little wonder that makos are referred to as 'blue dynamite with a short fuse'.

We hadn't been drifting long when a mako of about 250 pounds took a bait right at the back of the boat. I took the strike. It gave me a good fight for an hour or so, leaping all over the ocean before Jack finally gaffed it and secured it to the side of the boat.

The next strike was another mako of about 300 pounds, which Nicky took. After another hard fight of about half an hour, it too was captured, tail-roped and tied off a bollard.

Then another mako swam right up to the back of the boat and tried to eat the berley pot. It was a big bastard and it had its mouth around the stainless steel chum pot and was trying to wrench it from the boat.

Jack ran inside and got the Australian record chart. 'How big do you reckon that fish is, Paul?' he asked, knowing that I had seen more than my share of big makos over the years.

'I reckon 600 pounds would stop it cold, Jack,' I said as I admired the great fish's magnificent shades of blue and its superb shape – it could have been carved out of onyx. Dreading what was to come, I wondered if guided missiles had been designed with makos in mind.

I knew that soon I would probably be called upon to kill this beautiful eating machine. I hated doing it, but back in those kill-anything-that-swims days of the 1960s and 1970s it was my job ... and that was that.

'The Australian record for a mako on 20 pound line is just over 500 pounds, and this bloke is around 550 pounds,' Jack said as he threaded half a striped tuna onto a huge hook, attached it to a rod and reel fitted with 20 pound line and fed the bait down the big mako's crockery-encrusted craw. 'OK, let's get ourselves an Australian record that won't be beaten in a hurry.'

The Boss wasn't into catching sharks; he sat on the flying bridge, sipping on a Chivas, puffing away on a cigar, happily watching the activity and chatting with Gringo. He didn't give a damn about gamefishing. Next week he would catch some snappers.

Jack wound up the drag on the reel and sank the hook, expecting the big fish to take off. But it didn't budge. It just stayed where it was, munching on the berley pot and swimming from one side of the boat to the other.

'Piss off, you bastard,' Jack yelled at the shark, but it didn't. It just hung around the back of the boat, offering no resistance at all. So I prodded it with the blunt end of a boat hook. That did the trick, and with one almighty swish of its tail, which nearly drenched us, it took off like a burning dog.

Jack leaned on the rod in an effort to fight the fish, and after about 200 metres of line had disappeared off the reel it seemed he was winning. Then the line went slack. Jack wound as fast as he could, but he couldn't get fast to the fish again. We thought he had busted.

But no. 'The bloody thing's swimming back to the berley pot quicker than I can wind in the line,' Jack yelled in amazement as the mako materialised at the back of the boat, munching on the pot again, oblivious to the wire trace hanging out of its mouth. It didn't know that it was hooked.

'Get the gaff,' yelled Jack. 'It took enough line off the reel to be considered a legal catch. Gaff it.'

'Bullshit,' I said, 'are you crazy? Those things are mental enough at the gaff when they are exhausted after they've been fought for hours. Do you expect me to gaff one green?'

'Yes, so don't argue with me. Just do as you're told.'

I had no choice. That's the unwritten law of the ocean. The captain kicks the mate, the mate kicks the cabin boy and the cabin boy kicks the cat. Like it or lump it, on a boat you do as you're told. Even in fishing. I looked up at the Boss for a second opinion and maybe a bit of sympathy.

'Do as he bloody fuckin' says,' Theo the Boss growled, obviously unaware that in a minute I would be killed.

So I did as Jack commanded. I attached the end of the flying gaff rope to a bollard on the deck in the corner of the tuck, leaned over the back of the boat, placed the gaff head into the shark's shoulder just below the gills and pulled on the gaff pole and rope at the same time. The huge gaff hook went straight in.

None of us was prepared for what happened next. The water erupted as if a depth charge had gone off just below the surface. And as if gaining momentum to leap into the boat and bite my head off for sticking that mammoth gaff into it, the shark plunged as deep as the length of the 14 foot gaff rope would allow and then shot through the surface, leapt the full length of the rope in mid-air above our heads and came crashing down onto the transom of the boat, snapping, blurting, grunting and biting at anything within snapping distance. Curiously, at that moment of sheer terror, I can recall its breath. Yuk. It was vile.

Fortunately for us it fell out of the boat and not into the cockpit, but as it did, it lifted the gaff rope over my head and behind me, pinning me in the corner of the boat between the bollard and the fish going berserk on the end of the gaff rope. I was copping rope burns all over my legs and back as the fish lunged and jumped, trying to throw the gaff.

Theo the Boss was far from impressed with what was happening to his pride and joy, and was even less impressed when the huge fish started breaking its teeth on the marlin board and smashing holes in the polished fibreglass hull with its tail. Finally he'd had enough.

'Look what that bloody fuckin' bastard's doing to my bloody beautiful fuckin' boat. No bastard does that and fuckin' gets away with it. Gringo, shoot that fucker,' he screamed.

Although he didn't know it, the Boss had probably just put out the world's first contract on a shark. And Gringo didn't have to be told twice. He produced the huge cannon from inside his jacket and climbed down the flying bridge ladder, waving it in the air. As he hit the deck he aimed and took a shot at the shark as it propelled itself above the tuck of the boat.

I felt the bullet whistle past my ear – it missed the shark and landed in the water a hundred metres off the back of the boat. By this stage I had somehow managed to get the gaff rope over my head, but I was bloodied and bruised from head to foot. Nicky had broken a finger trying to get a tail rope on the shark and now we had a totally pissed-off shark and a gun-toting lunatic to contend with.

The Boss looked on at the mayhem below him and seemed to be enjoying it all. Just as Gringo was about to rattle off another shot, Jack called a halt to proceedings.

'Theo,' he called. 'You can't gaff a record fish with a .45 hand gun. It will be disqualified. If we take that fish in to weigh it and it has bullet holes in it there will be an uproar. Call Gringo off.'

The Boss listened to Jack and told Gringo to put the smoking gun away. Thank Christ for that. But we still had the shark to contend with. It was 45 minutes between when I gaffed it and when we ended up tying it to the side of the boat. We had been battered from one side of the boat to the other, and had the bruises and broken bones to prove it. Not to mention the near-death experience with a bullet.

The mako weighed 556 pounds – an Australian record for the time on 20 pound breaking strain line.